WOMEN
OF THE
CENTRE

Edited by ADELE PRING

Mumu handi bat.

Vicky

First published 1990
Second Printing 1992
by Pascoe Publishing Pty Ltd
P.O. Box 42, Apollo Bay 3233
Australia

Women of the Centre
ISBN 0 947087 23 0

Printed in Australia by
Australian Print Group, Maryborough
Typeset in Baskerville by Bookset
Cover graphics Stephen Pascoe
Cover art Dora Smith
Consultant Editors: Bruce Pascoe
                    Lyn Harwood

This project was assisted by the
Aboriginal Arts Committee of the
Australia Council, the Federal
Government Arts funding and
advisory body.

Contents

Acknowledgements

Lallie Lennon's story first appeared in *Australian Short Stories* no 12 (Pascoe Publishing 1985) and later *The Babe is Wise* (Pascoe Publishing). It was titled *Maralinga*. Muriel Olsson's story first appeared, titled *Ernabella Story*, in *Australian Short Stories* no 17 (Pascoe Publishing 1987). Miriam Dadleh's story first appeared in *Australian Short Stories* no 20 (Pascoe Publishing 1987). Milly Taylor's story first appeared in *Australian Short Stories* no 24 (Pascoe Publishing 1988).

Photographs reproduced with the kind permission of Len Beadell appear in the book *Still in the Bush* by Len Beadell, Rigby Publishers.

Introduction

These remarkable stories have two purposes: to help readers understand the lives of the storytellers, all of whom have lived in rural areas most of their lives like many other Australians, but whose lives have been very different to those of non-Aboriginal Australians, and to provide personal written histories for the descendants of the women involved.

I first met the women as an enthusiastic and, in retrospect, naive teacher of Aboriginal Studies at Augusta Park High School in Port Augusta. The Aboriginal community in Port Augusta had been involved in school programmes previously and I continued this very valuable liaison. When I first heard Aboriginal women telling stories of how they grew up, I realized what amazingly adaptable women they must be to live in two conflicting cultures so successfully and with so little bitterness and anger for the often dreadful things imposed on their lives. Not only did I feel the stories should be recorded but the women also wanted them recorded. They wanted their children and grandchildren to know about their lives and wanted others to understand as well.

Some of the women had overcome their bitterness through their involvement in religion. Others realized that they could be treated both badly and well by people of any race. They had come to judge all people as individuals.

Most of the storytellers share either the experience of being taken away from their families as children or living in fear of it happening. Muriel Olsson didn't see her mother from when she was an infant until she was a mother herself, by which time her own mother was elderly and frail and even then they could not speak to each other because they had no language in common. The government of the day ignored the wishes of the parents, especially the mothers, because they thought it best for the children to be removed and isolated from their families.

Audrey Kinnear was sent from the west coast to a boarding school in Adelaide and later trained as a nurse. She didn't meet her mother again for about twenty years and it has taken her many years to come to terms with her anguish. Audrey's sister, Lorna Grantham, lived an entirely different life which was semi-traditional. She married her promised husband, lived on bush tucker and kept her language and traditions. Their stories provide a moving contrast.

Ruth McKenzie had a very traumatic childhood. Her life has not been easy since but she wanted her story told so that people would know the truth. When she was a young child, her mother was killed by her stepfather under the requirements of Aboriginal law because Ruth accidentally saw part of a ceremony she wasn't supposed to have seen. She was soon after placed in the Oodnadatta Children's Home with missionaries. She still feels bitterness towards them because of the harsh way they raised children but feels bitterness at the cruelties too of Aboriginal law. She was sent to work in the Flinders Ranges where as a girl she had to chop railway sleepers for firewood and scrub floors until they shone — all for no payment. She married an Adnyamathanha man whose community cruelly rejected her because she was not one of them and because he'd been promised to someone else. Ruth has had thirteen children and now has many grandchildren.

Miriam Dadleh grew up mainly with her father who was Afghan and who travelled through the outback carrying goods on their camel train. Her mother died when she was a very young girl. Miriam felt the conflict of cultures with her father being Moslem and his prejudice against many Aboriginal people. Miriam had however talked with Aboriginal people during their travels and learnt their languages, much to her father's relief when they were lost in remote country one time. Miriam tells her story with lots of humour, even of the days when she was a drinker, smoker and gambler, none of which she indulges in now.

Milly Taylor has lived in many places, missions, stations and towns, yet retained her language and traditions. Despite the good relationship between her Aboriginal mother and Irish father the government made them separate. When Milly's father had to leave, the family moved to the mission at Ernabella but left to live off the land so that her mother could go back to her people's country. They had no clothes and weren't even allowed to drink from the wells sunk for cattle. They had to find rockholes in the hills.

Eva Strangways lived like many Aboriginal people at the time, travelling around on camel wagons while the men undertook stock and fencing work on stations. She still has her language and proudly teaches her grandchildren. Amazingly, she cannot recall ever feeling any prejudice against her.

Lallie Lennon's story is incredible. Her family were exposed to the fallout from the atomic bomb tests in the 1950's and she and her children still have associated illnesses from that time. She has never received any compensation. Like most Aboriginal people at the time, she had no understanding of what an atomic bomb was and for many years doctors would not accept that her family's sicknesses were caused by the black mist.

Jenny Grace is the youngest of the storytellers. She grew up in the 1950's on the River Murray. While it was economic boom times for most Australians, Jenny's family lived by trapping native water rats and selling their skins and by seasonal fishing, living much of the time in temporary shelters made from wheat bags sewn together and other times in a house made from recycled rubbish including kerosene cans. Little wonder that Jenny couldn't see the point of learning when she attended school because she thought her adult life would be the same as that of her parents. Jenny is now studying for her Diploma in Teaching as an adult student and is a mother to her own and foster children.

Faith Thomas has had a remarkable career including nursing in various Aboriginal communities, representing both South Australia and Australia in women's cricket and being the state's first Aboriginal public servant. She admits to being a spoilt brat as a child and tells her story with lots of humour.

The silk-screen print on the cover is by Dora Smith, a young mother and Ngarrindjeri woman from Berri. The baby in the print is her daughter, Nina. Her inspiration was to blend traditional themes with the present.

I would like to thank the storytellers, their families and communities and in particular the Aboriginal students who assisted in recording and interviewing, including Lana Grantham, Janeane Dadleh, Tanya Bodger, Anndrina Kartinyeri, Melissa Strangways, Lavenia Dadleh, Peter Kafetsis, Peter Willis, Michelle Wright, Elizabeth Trench, Johnny Butler, Kevin Buzzacott and others. Without them, this publication would not have happened. I also appreciate the assistance given by the South Australian Jubilee 150 committee, Augusta Park High School, Chris Warren, Heather Stuart and the Aboriginal Studies Team in the Education Department of South Australia.

I would also like to thank those who assisted in locating photographs, including the women, some of whom had family photos; Len Beadell who took photographs while working near Woomera in the 1950's; and Ron Lister who has collected many photographs which were taken in Ernabella in the early days.

Adele Pring

Map showing the traditional country of the storytellers

NORTHERN TERRITORY

QUEENSLAND

WESTERN AUSTRALIA

West Aranda

Aluritja

East Aranda

Pitjantjatjara

Antikirinja

Yankunytjatjara

Arabana

Kookatha

Adnyamathanha

SOUTH AUSTRALIA

NEW SOUTH WALES

Ngarrindjeri

VICTORIA

The Women's Traditional Groups

Miriam Dadleh	Aranda
Jenny Grace	Ngarrindjeri
Lorna Grantham	Pitjantjatjara/Yankunytjatjura
Audrey Kinnear	Pitjantjatjara/Yankunytjatjura
Lallie Lennon	Yankunytjatjara
Ruth McKenzie	Aranda/Aluritja
Muriel Olsson	Yankunytjatjara
Eva Strangways	Antikirinja/Kookatha
Milly Taylor	Antikirinja
Faith Thomas	Adnyamathanha

Boundaries between Aboriginal groups have not been drawn on this map. Their country is indicated by where their name has been placed. Tindale and others have attempted to draw lines on maps and his work is as accurate as anyone's but even his boundaries have been disputed.

Muriel Olsson

Muriel lived until she was five with her Yankuntjatjara mother and English father near Ernabella in the north-west after which she and her sisters were taken and placed in Colebrook Home at Quorn and later Eden Hills in Adelaide. She later qualified as a nurse, married and had four children to her Swedish husband. She has lived sometime in Sweden. After her own children were born, Muriel traced her mother who was quite frail and still sad at having lost her children so many years before. Muriel lived in Quorn and Port Augusta for many years but lives now between Adelaide and Mimili where she works with her people.

From the Heart

I 'll go back to the time I lived at Ernabella — actually it was Shirley Well which was between Ernabella and Fregon that my mother and I lived together with my other sisters — that was in about 1936 — I can remember back to that time.

Every now and again the police would come and they'd take kids away to different places but this particular time it was Oodnadatta where there was a mission home run by the United Aborigines Mission. There was a missionary there by the name of Miss Amery — a really beautiful lady. But the bush telegraph would usually get to work before the police got to the communities and mothers would hide their children right, left and centre; but for some reason we happened to be in Ernabella at that time and six of us, my two sisters, myself and three cousins — we were all taken away. My mother came with us to the mission at Oodnadatta but I don't ever remember what happened to her when we got there — she just sort of disappeared into thin air — never saw her again. When I say never, I mean up until 1968 — that was the next time I saw her.

We had to learn to live in a house and in a bed and know how to eat with knives and forks and what have you — wear clothes and all those new things. I think a very traumatic thing was the fact that we were lying in these very high beds. We didn't have the closeness — the warmth of the earth — the closeness of our relatives around us and a little small area with a fire in front of it. Everyone had to sleep in separate beds — that was too strange and very frightening — the height to start with and being separated from one another. Then our cousins — the three of them — were put in another room.

One of my cousins and I, I used to call her Kantja, her name was Grace, decided we were going to run back to Ernabella. We didn't get too far, as I told people before — we came across the steam train and that frightened the living daylights out of us — we thought it was a mamu so we ran as fast as our legs would carry us back to the mission the only place of safety we knew.

There were some lovely things — remembering back to Ernabella and the places up in the north-west — the absolute beauty of the country and the landscape are the things that go very deep into the heart. I remember as a little kid I used to get up before dawn and lay up on the rocks overlooking the waterhole where the brumbies used to come and water — and how the stallions used to lead the mares — it was a really magnificent sight — I never forgot that. The appreciation of beauty is something that goes very deep when you're amongst it from the beginning of your life. For me I think that's the reason that I don't criticise — you know how a lot of people say the missionaries have done this and done that — but I can only be very thankful myself because I don't believe that anything in life comes without a purpose. It's how you handle a situation and how you take hold of it — use it for good — what was meant for evil — that you can look at it and see the good that it has done. That for me is a very real thing.

I guess the government didn't mean it as something bad — it's just the fact that our mothers weren't treated as human beings and people having feelings — naturally a mother's got a heart that is concerned for her children. For them to be taken away — without consultation; nobody can ever know the heartache. In those days the communication was so bad you didn't ever hear (well when I say that, I've since heard that people did come and sort of watch over the house and so on — people from our tribe) that somehow or other they always got word back. My mother said that the first time we saw her again she cried every day, because my name had been changed she always heard about the others but never heard my name and she said that every morning as the sun rose — she'd cry, (they'd all wail) — all those years until she saw us again. What a terrible thing that human beings do that kind of thing to each other.

A lot of heartache for the mother not knowing where

the kids are — like I say communications were bad — there wasn't anything really except for the mail that went out — not until Flynn's overland telegraph — I don't know what year that was — it was a lot later.

I had a big sister, her name was Eileen, but her name was changed again because there was another Eileen in the home — her name was changed to Aileen. She was already working when we left Ernabella, working in one of the homesteads so she could speak a little bit of English. When we went to school — there were about four or five of us who started together — we could discuss what the teacher was saying because Aileen sort of gave us a bit of help. It was only my young sister, my baby sister who didn't go.

Our people are very religious people — very spiritual people and for myself I believe that going into a mission and learning about the Christian way of life held no conflict. It was a continuation of what was already here — of appreciating the land and walking on it and travelling with my mother on the camels and all that kind of thing, and just drinking in the wonder of it. It's just a part of your life — so I can understand — I just knew that one day I'd get back there — even though I was so young when I went into the home. We had to learn lots of scriptures — learn them off by heart — we did that too — because if we learnt them off by heart we could go out to play (laughs) so we learnt them off like parrots. But I tell you, in later years it comes back and it has the desired effect — comfort or whatever you need — so all is not lost.

I was about 5 when I was taken away, Eileen was about 3 or 4 years older than me and she was working in someone's home. Nancy had already come down when she was about 3 because she had infantile paralysis and there was our little sister who was about 3 years younger.

Gracie was one of my cousins — she came in with her two brothers. She became a double certificate nurse. Her sister Nellie became the first trained Aboriginal nurse in South Australia but she didn't do her training here — she had to go to Victoria to the Salvation Army hospital — Bethesda Hospital in Melbourne. Young

Aboriginal people were having problems at that time about getting employment and all that kind of thing — the young boys not being able to go into the armed forces if they wanted to — a whole heap of other things. We were just expected to be servants and stockmen. In August of 1953, with the help of the Aboriginal Advancement League, all the teenagers got together and had this meeting in the Adelaide Town Hall, and the press came in and it was from there that things began to change.

Some of the young boys spoke, it was all teenagers that did it you see — there was a real hue and cry in South Australia because people didn't know about our difficulties. So many people took so many things for granted back to that time — they thought everyone had equal rights and that wasn't so. I suppose it's just the fact that with our white friends and others, it probably didn't dawn on them that once we left school the same opportunities wouldn't be open to us as it was to them. Anyway I think that was a sort of turning point when people took up the hue and cry — said how disgraceful it was, in regard to South Australia that the first Aboriginal sister had to be trained outside of South Australia. It was from that particular meeting that young people were able to go into all kinds of trades, nursing and more or less anything they chose to be. That was the turning point.

Gracie's still nursing over in Melbourne. She was at the Aboriginal Medical Service there at Fitzroy at one stage but I think she's working at another hospital — I don't know where it is. Nellie was the one who was the matron up at Gumeracha. After I'd left school I went to work with a doctor and his wife to look after their little one. Years later Nellie asked me if I'd like to go up there with her. I eventually did that and I've been nursing ever since then. There again I suppose it's having someone to look up to — I guess I was very fortunate in that I had her to sort of ease me into a different kind of living. Having once been taken away from our people — when you left the home and left so many — you were sort of going back into the same sort of situation. You were just afloat — you had nothing to hang onto and that's a pretty big thing at 14 or whatever age I was. I was out in the world on my own with a little suitcase with one change of clothes, two sets of clothes to my name — that's all I had in the world. That was from 1946 to January 1947. See it wasn't until years after I left the home that I took up nursing.

The two old ladies of the mission saw us all the way through our lives, even though they left Colebrook and just took girls in at Parkside. They left Colebrook Home in Eden Hills when the government took over management. When Colebrook Home was in Quorn we didn't have discrimination with regard to schooling and that kind of thing but as soon as we got down to Adelaide there was a big petition going around at Eden Hills where Colebrook Home had moved to. Parents didn't want their children to be mixing with black kids. We'd never come across discrimination. Okay, we used to fight with the white kids and call them all kinds of things and they'd call us all kinds of things but it wasn't done in any nasty way. You had your fight and it was over and you were friends again. It was nothing other than that.

So at Eden Hills the Education Department gave us one teacher and we had school in one big room at the home which was made into a classroom. She had from grade 1 to grade 7. Kids that came after that didn't have the same good basic education that we did because we could just twist that lovely lady around our finger. When we didn't feel like doing what we were supposed to do, like when it was a beautiful day, we used to go out and look for all the different kinds of beautiful orchids around Eden Hills. We'd talk her into taking us out. We loved to sing too and her husband was a choir master so we'd sing our lives away and walk all over the countryside. She was very good at handicrafts — teaching us handicrafts and that kind of thing. Us older ones had a good basic education at Quorn. I'd done all the primary up to grade 6 at that time — I just had grade 7 at Eden Hills, then went down to the Girls Tech in Unley but the others who came after that hadn't had a good solid grounding in schooling. It really told on them in later life when they became adults. Of course some who were very determined in doing the kinds of things they wanted to do by recording it on tape — you know lectures on tape and all that kind of thing — because they had the will they came through it and educated themselves you might as well say. I don't want to put her (the teacher) down — because she was a really lovely person. It was too much — the Education Department should have been made aware of it.

I was at Quorn until grade 6. In 1943 we went down to Eden Hills in Adelaide for a holiday because there had been drought for I don't know how many years. We used the last drop of water the day we left — we had one of those great underground tanks with a hand pump. We used the last lot for a cup of tea and we left. We never ever thought we weren't going to come back. We'd hidden all our little treasures in different places but we never ever went back to Quorn to get them. We stayed up at Eden Hills and went to school from there.

When we were in the Quorn home, there were other girls and boys there. Danny Colson, Ruth McKenzie. I know there are quite a lot of people when you stop and count them — a lot of people who went through Colebrook Home. A lot of people who did very well too — I think that's how we were brought up. That's why I get really cranky when I hear people criticising the missionaries — they taught us to be independent and anything that was worth getting, was worth working for, and I believe I've got them to thank for that kind of thinking — you don't have things put in your lap — but you've got to do something about working to get whatever you want.

Some of the kids at Colebrook were quite a lot older when they were brought to the home and had a bit of trouble with school and learning English. Danny's cousin came in about the same time — she was about 14 and I think it would have been very hard for her. I think Danny would have been about 11 but Ruby was just that much older. She was very, very tall which made it hard to start in grade 1 — it must have been traumatic. She used to be ill a lot — severe headaches and so on —

migraines. I would say that they had their origins in stress and the fact that she couldn't talk to anyone about it, how to cope with it or how to go about coming to grips with it. When you're younger you can adjust better — more quickly and just take life as it comes — day after day — but see Ruby already knew the tribal ways — so it must have been really hard for her.   She's gone back to her people's country now to live. She's got her homeland so it's really good — she's on the Council and able to help to give the people an understanding of the kinds of things they need to know for meetings. There never can be a going back — you can't ever regain what's lost — you've got to make the most of what's here right now.

It was forbidden for us to talk in our own language. If we had been allowed we would have retained it. We were forbidden to speak it. I think that's the one criticism I'd make of the missionaries because when you lose your language you've lost part of yourself; communicating is very important.

After Colebrook Home shifted from Oodnadatta to Quorn we were so far removed that we were cut off completely. We weren't allowed to talk about anything that belonged to our tribal life. I suppose they more or less told us we had to become white people — I don't hold that as a criticism neither — I just say that human beings, being what we are, can make mistakes even though you think it's going to be for good — but you make mistakes that later on you can regret. The missionary women had a really deep love and respect for our people otherwise they couldn't have gone up there — living with camels and camping out. In history books people say that we were wild savages but the missionary women went and they camped amongst the people — they lived with our people — they didn't live in town with the other white people — not until they got a tin shed and bought that for the kids who didn't have any parents or for kids whose parents wanted them educated by the missionaries. That's how the home was started.

We'd just been taken from one situation to another — first of all three or four hundred miles away to Oodnadatta and then all that distance on the train down to Quorn. We didn't know what was going on so the six of us would just go down and sit on the bank of the creek and wail and cry and cut our feet with sharp stones. We'd just wail for what we had lost I guess. I remember really clearly that we did that. I guess that's what it was — didn't any longer have familiar things around and didn't have a mother there to comfort us. Being forty kids in a home I think you conditioned yourself to the fact that they couldn't listen to you and you had to try and solve everything yourself — or talk to our own peer group. We were divided into age groups but kids your own age aren't any wiser than you are.

They used to cane us a lot. Never hurt anybody — I think it's the lack of it that hurts people and that's obvious today. I just can't understand it — the way kids talk to teachers nowadays — there again it's a different age and I suppose the teachers commanded respect but things are more open now. In those days teachers might have done things that you could criticise them for but you never ever saw it. They were sort of on a pedestal.

In Quorn we walked two miles to school. It was good fun walking. On the way we'd go chasing kangaroos or emus or whatever, we'd talk and tell stories — it wasn't a long way — sometimes it went very quickly — too short really.

In later years when I went back to Ernabella we gathered the seeds again to make damper. As I gathered it and tasted it, all the tastes came back to me — you know all the different things like the honey ants, the witchettys and all the different kinds of food — the wild tomatoes, wild gooseberries — oh lovely — beautiful taste — it's really good.

After school I went to work as a maid for a doctor and his wife — they had one little girl — I more or less brought her up. I worked there until November 1948 or 1949 and then my cousin who was the matron up at Gumeracha Hospital wanted nurses to train, so I went up there. I was very shy and so lacking in confidence that I didn't get through the exams at all — not until many years after because I used to be so frightened that

19

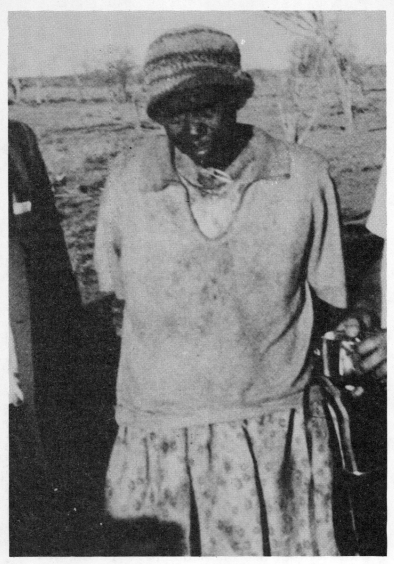

Munyi, Muriel's mother, whom she hadn't seen since 1936 when she and her sisters were taken away. Muriel found her again only when she was a mother of four herself.
Munyi lived for only a short time after Muriel got to know her again.

Paddy Uluru, Muriel's stepfather who was a traditional owner of Ayers Rock (Uluru). He has now passed away.

I'd just go totally blank. I knew in my heart that I had a lot more in my head than a lot of girls who were getting through so I never gave up. I kept on trying and then after the 1953 meeting the opportunity came for us to start at the Royal Adelaide. I didn't go in straight away — I didn't start until 1956 — I went to Bible College after that 1953 meeting. I went to Bible College for 2 years and then when I finished I went to Royal Adelaide and from there to the Queen Vic to do a midwifery course.

After I left the Queen Vic I went apple-picking over in Tasmania. It was a lovely place. I'd been there before because in our first year of nursing we hiked all around. A couple of my friends and I joined the Youth Hostels and walked all around — really beautiful place — lovely people.

I met my husband there. He is Swedish. Our two eldest children were born in Sweden — so they're Swedes. They became Australian citizens in November 1986.

We lived in Sweden for about five years. It was good. Bengt's people were mainly country people so it was really good. It's a beautiful country, beautiful people so it was good.

They knew nothing about Australia. It's amazing — but there again they learnt a lot about their own land and I think sometimes that can be neglected — pride in your own — I think that's a really important thing — and pride in what you are — pride in your own land. Like I said I always knew that I'd go back and I always knew one day I'd do something for my own people. It took longer than I expected but I believe it's always at the right time — when you've had experience of life and your life's been formed so that you're better able to do the things that are most helpful — when you can give the most out of life's experiences I suppose.

We came back from Sweden in 1965. My husband went to see my white father Alan Brumby in Alice Springs and said 'I'm your son-in-law,' and he didn't know quite where to look and my husband said, 'I'd like photos of you so I can show my children'—but my father made sure that

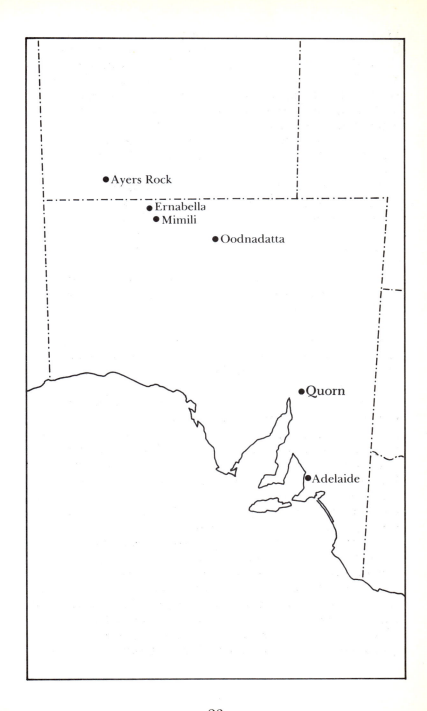

• Ayers Rock

• Ernabella
• Mimili

• Oodnadatta

• Quorn

• Adelaide

in the photos that he gave, his face was shaded over by big hats. That's the kind of thing I've talked about before — about learning how to forgive when the hurt is so deep — learning how to forgive because it's only through forgiving that you yourself come alive. You can't live with hatred and hurting eating you out or bitterness of any kind. That's just my experience of life. Unless you get rid of that bitterness and hatred and whatever that's bugging you — you can only be a half a person — you can only be — not the person that you should be — could be. It was not until recently when I was talking to an old auntie that I learned that I could be proud of my white heritage too. The antagonism I had for my father is gone. I have heard he was a good man. I can see things differently now and I'm glad. It has made everything more complete — made my understanding more complete.

It was soon after that, 1968, that I saw my mother, first time since 1936.

We just stood and couldn't understand a word — it was the cruellest thing. I don't know if I would have been brave enough if I'd known it was going to be like that — if I'd known it was going to cut so deep — but I'm really glad I did for the sake of the kids because they really love their family up there. Annika especially had a really special bond with her grandmother — it was something beautiful to see when she'd go into the wurlie and bath her grandmother — because my mother was very ill when we got back — so Annika would go and bath her and make her more comfortable — shake her mattress — sweep out her little wurlie — feed her with soup and soft things.

Mimili — that's our home area — that's where my family group live around that part. My father owns all that Ayers Rock area — my step-father — he's the only father I've ever known so he deserved the name of father. We went with him up to Ayers Rock and he was able to take us all the way around and explain and show us different things and the reason that he was entrusted with Ayers Rock to look after.

I go up every year if I can — it's really good and more

24

and more you can understand — each time you can understand more.

1975 was about the last time we saw my mother — went up there in January — left here the day after Christmas I think it was and I think she died in that Easter time — Thursday before Good Friday.

Couple of my sisters have only been back to our homelands a few times — but let's say the Aborigine is in me more than the rest of them. I think that probably a lot of Aboriginal people have been made to feel ashamed of what they are. I think people really succeeded in making you feel like that and that's another really traumatic thing that you had to cope with when you grew up, that you wanted to go back to your own but you didn't sort of know how to go about it without the language and with that feeling also that you didn't know quite what to expect because of the kinds of things you'd been fed on. Wondering also how your relatives would feel and receive you.

But they want us to go back — because they have confidence in Clara and me in particular because we always go back. They want us to go back and stay and help but you've got to work out where you can be most helpful. I think this particular time — it's here in Port Augusta — I'm trying to get this health service set up and I'll train these young ones to make them aware of Aboriginal people as people — that's the most important thing. People don't behave the way they do with drinking and whatever without a very good reason for it — that dignity's been stripped off. Particularly that applies to the men when they can't provide for their families. Just now I think that the white people might be able to understand when their kids can't get a job — they might begin to understand a little bit of what our people have had to put up with all their lives. That might give them a little bit of understanding when they've got to go through the same trauma. On leaving school, you're not assured of a job anymore, but that's been our life — all our life. You have got to make something of yourself — but you can't do it on your own. My faith got me through.

Kids of today in high school have got to be determined if they want to get somewhere with their lives. I
think that goes for everybody — it's up to you what you
make of your opportunities. I guess we got it easy in that
we had to go home and we had to sit down and we had
to do our lessons and put a lot of pride into it. You were
marked on how you did your homework and how you
set it out and all that kind of thing. You couldn't do
anything slip-shod. But now a lot of kids have got
parents who can barely make themselves understood in
English, especially out at the Reserve so it's no wonder
kids are going right through primary, right through
high school and they can't really write adequately. What
I was referring to is if kids need help in English or they
need help in Mathematics — their parents can't help
them because they have come out of tribal situations.
The kids are really not coping. I can understand if they
fall so far behind that they feel as though they're never
going to catch up. They need support in being prepared
for a life in a changing Australia.

Faith Thomas

Faith's mother was an Adnyamathanha woman from the Flinders Ranges and her father was European. Under pressure, Faith's mother placed her as a baby in Colebrook Children's Home in Quorn. Faith, like Audrey and Muriel, also went on to qualify as a nurse. She has played test cricket for Australia against England and worked for both Aboriginal affairs and as a community health nurse in a range of Aboriginal communities in South Australia. Faith now lives at Quorn where she is actively involved in re-establishing Colebrook Home as a place for those who once lived there to return to, either permanently or for holidays.

From the Shoulder

I was two weeks old when I was placed in the Colebrook Children's Home at Quorn, but not where it is now, it was on a hill before. That one got too small so we moved when a bloke called Colebrook bought the property out past Stoney Creek. When I was about nine, we all shifted to Colebrook Home at Eden Hills.

How I came to be living in Quorn again as an adult was when my old man (my husband) retired, he got a bit disillusioned. I'd met him up in the Northern Territory. He was a Welshman. One time he was in charge of all the earth-moving equipment that was putting Pichi Richi pass through from Port Augusta to Quorn so he spent a lot of time up here and got to like the joint. I'd come up from Adelaide where we lived then and stay at the pub and the company would pay for that. When he wanted to sell down there in Adelaide, I said 'Well, where do you want to settle?' and he said 'Well, I sort of fell in love with Quorn.' It was his decision which was great. I felt really great coming back.

I've got very fond memories of the home. I always thank God I was brought up there. As far as I was concerned it was absolutely beautiful because I was the pet. My mother never lost contact with me and she would come and visit probably about every two or three years so I knew who my mum was. My old uncles and aunties used to come and stay with me at Eden Hills too, like Uncle Andy and others. They were regular visitors. My mum lived at Broken Hill.

When mum left Nepabunna, she rang Sister Hyde from the children's home to come and pick me up at Copley, so Sister Hyde jumped the train and went up there and mum and Bill, my brother went through. It's pretty ironic really because she got a job with a professor at Eden Hills as a housegirl and it was only three houses away from where we lived in Wilpena Street.

When Stuart (my son) started his schooling at Eden Hills, he sat at this desk and carved into it was 'Bill Coulthard' (my brother's name).

From what I hear from the old people, mum was booted out of Nepabunna. It was alright when Bill was born, the father was a bloke called Ted who was a mail driver but when the girl came along, she was booted out with her two kids. She had nothing else but to ring Sister Hyde and I was put in there. The kids named me Faith. Mum said, 'She's your girl now, you name her' and evidently the kids say that I was a little pip squeak and they said 'If it's going to survive, it'll have to be by faith, so we'll call her Faith.' It was the Faith Mission.

Mum always brought me shoes and socks or whatever and then when I started work, I used to go and visit her in Broken Hill.

Lois O'Donoghue and I were the same age. There were more of us the same age. Lois will tell you "bloomin' pet, she gets shoes and I never. She got this, I never." I got belted, she never. We went to school in Quorn and then there was a drought and we went to Eden Hills for our holidays and Sister Hyde said 'I'm not taking the kids back' because when we finished school, we'd have to cart water and Sister Hyde would be down the well getting water and we'd have to cart it across about half a mile with big buckets and Sister Rutter would put it in a tank on the back verandah. The night before we left we all had to get in and out of the same bath. The big ones first, the little ones got in and out of mud and there was enough water left for Sister Hyde and Sister Rutter to have their 'cuppa' in the morning before we caught the train. Sister Hyde said 'There's no way we're taking the kids back there.' In those days, Aborigines weren't allowed south of Gawler unless they had special permission.

We weren't allowed to go to school when we got down there to Eden Hills. They sent the Red Cross ladies to teach us. That's, I think, when I first realised we were different. Because why couldn't we go to school? We used to get these Red Cross ladies around the corner and belt hell out of them and they stopped coming. It lasted about a month and they all left with red crosses all over them. I think we were taking our anger out. 'Why can't we go to school? Why do we always have to have second best? Why should we have second best?' Then Sister Hyde took us. Poor thing. She was only a missionary. She'd give you a spelling test like 'knives' and we'd say 'What Sister Hyde?' and she'd say 'k-n-i-v-e-s.' She'd spell it for us.

Eventually, there was a whole lot of wrangles going on underneath, I've got some very interesting information from a book I dug up in the archives. Eventually, the Education Department brought up these grotty old desks and an old teacher who was due for retirement, an old girl called Mrs Freebee who taught grade 1 to 7. We thought we'd do the same to her but she became our best mate. We all fell in love with her and she lived just up the road. Her husband got terribly involved and started a choir and all that. She was absolutely brilliant.

After I got married, Sister Hyde and Sister Rutter lived with me. Stuart was lucky because he had his 'nannas' and then she lived with us in Quorn too.

When we were kids in Quorn we used to tease the Catholic kids. 'Catholic kids and hungry frogs' we used to call or something like that. We'd fight on the golf course after school. We'd get them down there and belt hell out of them. Gavin Kenneally, (Member of Parliament now) poor little bugger, he was only a little bloke, we used to get him. He was a 'Catholic frog.' He always laughs about that now, I only saw him the other day. He said, 'I'm still looking for Jessie Finnis.'

Jessie was a real wild blackfella. There was a whole lot of them came in about the same time. They couldn't speak English. They came in with only first names so the Sisters named them from wherever they came, like David Willoughby came from Mt Willoughby Station. He found out after he left the home that his name was Branson and he changed it back. Ruby Musgrave came from the Musgrave Ranges. Jessie Finnis came from Finnis Springs. I always used to say 'Thank God, they knew my name was Faith Coulthard, I would have been Faith Nepabunna!'

I used to be a little bugger at school. I used to head

Girls in Colebrook Home uniform, outside laundry, 2nd home at Quorn. 1939
Middle Row: Faith Coulthard, Lois O'Donoghue, Muriel Brumby, Amy O'Donoghue.

From left to right Faith, Sister Hyde, Sister Rutter (the missionaries who ran the Colebrook Home) and Muriel Brumby (Olsson).

for Devil's Peak (a rugged mountain near Quorn in the Flinders Ranges) and catch up with the other kids on the way home from school because when I went to school, I'd get into trouble all the time. I didn't like school. Anything could have happened, I could've got bitten by a snake. No-one dobbed. Mum was the word.

Those were the days of the depression and the war was on and you had bells ringing all over the place and you'd go to ground. You had trenches and everything and you had to go and find a safe place to hide all around the town. The favourite places were under the fig trees or in the gutter in front of the baker's shop to see if you were going to get a bun. Never in a trench though or anything like that. I think Lois was the only one who had any nouse — she'd run to the doctor's place. We were only thinking of the tucker.

I can remember at the Home, Sister Hyde saying 'We haven't got any food — let's ask the Lord to provide' so we'd get on our knees and pray. Next thing there was a knock at the door. 'Sister Hyde, I've got fifty loaves of bread left over, would you like them?' Then we'd have to get on our knees and thank the Lord for that. Another knock on the door and the old butcher would come across 'Sister Hyde, I've got some fat, would you like it?' Fart he used to call it. We'd cut the meat off it and stew it. And the green grocer too because there weren't any cool rooms or things like that to keep the vegetables fresh.

The time we ate best was when the troop trains were coming through. We'd whiz out of school and stand down there on the crossing. 'Welcome to Quorn' we'd say and the CWA used to feed the soldiers on the lawn down opposite the crossing. 'Welcome to Quorn' and they'd be chucking out their tins of bully beef, sausages and vegetables and we'd go down and get our nails in the creek (to open the cans), sit down and have a good feed. When the train didn't come in, then all the tucker would come out to us at the home. It was the first time I'd seen salad. We'd get all this flash soldier's tucker.

When it was harvest festival time at the church, they'd send all the fruit and vegetables up, but by the time they finished, about half of them were rotten anyhow. So they were the times when we had ample food.

I wasn't conscious of being an Adnyamathanha person when I was young. No-one pointed it out. Nothing worried me. I was just a spoilt little brat. The first two of my relatives I saw were Uncle Sandy and Uncle Tim. Uncle Tim had just come back from the war and had his army uniform on and one brought the biggest packet of jelly beans and the other one gave me two pounds. That went to the kids for the holidays that we used to have down south. I was proud of my two uncles. I didn't know they was Adnyamathanha, they were just my two uncles and they had a uniform on. They were soldiers. Then they went away. That was my first contact apart from my mum.

I always said, my last job would be amongst my own mob, the Adnyamathanha mob, and then I finish and that's what I did. I worked up around Nepabunna as a nurse for a couple of years. I realize now that in a way it was good but in another it wasn't because I'd be on the run the whole time, I just knew them as my patients. I didn't have time to sit and have a cuppa. We had our week patrol which went from here (Quorn) to Marree and Moolawatana, sometimes back stations, and back again, so it was hit and run.

I never had an exemption certificate. That was a certificate which declared you a *non-Aborigine*, kind of like *honorary white*. Without it you couldn't have a bank account, buy land or drink. The Protector of Aborigines thought I needed one. I was the first public servant and I was working in Kintore Avenue. I only wish I could find that bloomin' letter I wrote. There was a bloke called Clarrie Bartlett and I was an embarrassment being an Aboriginal in the Department. It was the Department of Aboriginal Affairs and we were with the fire service. We had a fleet of three cars. He had a big grey Customline and we had a Holden and there was a Morris. There was Jill Thompson, Marj Angas and Gerta Martinow, myself, Clarrie Miller and Mr Copley. We were all welfare officers. Bill Wedding was the accountant and he played football for Norwood, and we had two typists.

This was in the days of the exemptions, so old Clarrie said to me one day 'I think it's time you got an exemption.' I said 'I don't want an exemption, Mr Bartlett.' 'Why not?' I said 'I'm a person. A piece of paper is not going to make me a better person.' So every morning I'd get dragged into his office and he'd go through this and I'd just sit there and wouldn't say anything. He'd go and get Marj and say 'You talk to her, you might be able to get through to her. She's gone Abo on me.' So Marj and I used to sit and laugh about it. 'She's gone Abo!'

He called me in one day and said 'I'm going to give you an honorary exemption, right?' He was going to get the board to give me an honorary exemption. I said 'If you do, Mr Bartlett, I'll write a letter to the paper and say this thing was forced on me.' I never got my exemption, did I, because I was going to go public if they dared.

People seemed pretty happy in Adelaide. I know because I was looking after them. They'd come to the counter and they'd say 'This is better than the reserve. We've got facilities here and we can stay with our relations and at least we can get on with living our own lives.' It wasn't all good though.

When I was at the Adelaide Hospital as a nurse, police would pull my mates up and chat to them about consorting with an Aboriginal. Our money was paid into a bank in Rundle Street and on our day off we'd go and get our money, go to the pictures and to the Quality Inn for a feed and have crumbed brains or whatever. It was a downstairs inn in Grenfell Street, all blue and white.

I went nursing after I worked for the Department of Aboriginal Affairs. How that came about was first of all I started off at Lush Studios because I wanted to be a commercial artist seeing I couldn't be a policewoman. I didn't want to be in the police when it came to the crunch. It was only a dream I had when I was a school kid. You know when they pass those little slips around and ask what you want to be? I wanted to be a policewoman or a carpenter. So I went and worked for this bloke called Lyall Lush. He used to put out all these Sunday School tickets. When you got twelve, you got a

34

bigger one. We were in cohorts with Atkinsons. We used to tint his race horse pictures. I used to get thirty bob ($3.00) a week. My train ticket was fifteen bob a week, my board was ten bob a week which meant I had five bob a week. I thought stuff this. In my holidays, I used to work testing eggs for Farmers' Union, making jam for IXL and all things like that just so I could buy a dress.

Sister Hyde had a sewing machine, she was a dressmaker and a milliner. I've still got her old sewing machine here, it dates back to Colebrook.

Getting back to that exemption thing, they had a book in the office with the names of the blackfellas who were exempted and if, say the boys came in from the shearing shed with their mates and wanted a few beers, the publican would ring up and say, 'Now this Tommy Dodd, is he exempted?' 'Just a minute,' I'd say. So I'd go out to the toilet and wander around, come back and say, 'Are you still there? Yes, he is, no worries. Can I talk to him.' I'd get on the phone and say, 'Now listen Tommy, you're not bloody exempted, just don't make a fool of yourself or I'll cop it.' I didn't last there that long anyhow.

Then I went to university for a year and I don't know why I went there. I played a lot of cricket, a lot of hockey and a lot of squash. I don't even know what course I was doing. I think I went to two lectures. Whatever I wanted to do I did. I was stuck in St Anne's College and I was one of the seniors out there. The other senior was Gwen Woods. Now Gwennie Woods and I went to school together here in Quorn. She'd finished her nursing. She was at Wakefield Street but we'd never lost contact and then she decided she'd go on and do her doctoring. She's up at Kimba at the present time. She was always a brilliant student here at Quorn. One thing we had over her was we always had to march into school and poor old Gwen when she marched, she'd march with her legs apart; so it didn't matter if she beat us with her school work, we could march! We used to make her open the windows and we'd hide the pole to make it hard for her. Gwen would be standing there showing her bell-bottomed bloomers and we'd laugh our heads off. Little things that stick in your mind, eh?

So I went to uni and I think they kicked me out. I suppose you'd call it kicking you out if they said 'don't worry about coming back.' I don't know where in the hell I was working next but there was Lois and Grace and Muriel (all from Colebrook Home). They all wanted to go nursing. We came along to the interview and of course Nellie Lester, (she couldn't do her nursing training in South Australia, she went to Bethesda in Victoria,) she said when you talk to matron, just stand with your hands behind your back. So I went along for the ride. We get into the revolving door in Brice Building and didn't know how to get out, we'd just go around and around in circles. A little mob of blackfellas running around, eyes this big. It eventually spewed us out, some back out where they came from and some back into the corridor. So we got to matron's office. She came out and we were sitting in this pew. We got up and said 'Good morning' and she didn't even invite us into her office. She told us to get back to Alice Springs and nurse our own people. So we headed back to Kintore Avenue and saw the Protector of Aborigines. It wasn't Bartlett then, it was the one before him. I'm getting my story upside down, but still . . .

Then we went over and saw Dr Duguid, who was in the Aboriginal Friends Association. They had this massive meeting in the Adelaide Town Hall about it and that hall was bloody packed. The Colebrook kids got up and sang their hymns and some of the old sisters were there and they said 'If you girls want to go nursing, go out to country hospitals, because she can't knock back a transfer.' So I went to Murray Bridge. Lois and Grace went to Victor Harbor. Muriel went to Angaston and Margaret went to Gumeracha or somewhere. We all transferred on that same idea and she couldn't do a bloody thing about it. That wasn't the first fight.

When I was up at Alice Springs, they'd say 'Where's that Aboriginal sister?' 'Who?' and they'd really have to stop and think who was that Aboriginal sister. I was just Faith, their mate. You find that particularly in the country hospitals. You all stick together. You're a unit. You're not black, you're not white, you're nothing, you're just a nurse. You find that with people that you work with in little communities. In those days there were no blackfellas in Murray Bridge, not like there are now.

I did about two years at Murray Bridge and then transfered to the Adelaide and then went straight from there to the Queen Liz and did my midwifery and from there straight to Point McLeay because I thought 'I can't stand four walls, I hate it.' I created my job here in the Flinders. I had to create it so I could have it but I did that Amata one, that was good, but I left up there when the little fella (my son) had to start kindergarten. I used to cart him on patrol here. The old man was a mechanic up there and then we got a transfer down to Point Pearce so he could start kindy. That's where he started his schooling. I've been to all the communities bar the west coast mob or the south east.

I had a few battles in nursing. I'd go to wash a patient and they might say 'Get your hands off me you bloody black bastard'. So a bit of metho used to get splashed where it wasn't supposed to. Matron did her round at eleven o'clock every morning and in those days medical wards were long and had about sixty patients. I'd get a message. Could Nurse Coulthard come and see me at half past eleven please. So off I'd go and get this bloody lecture on tolerance. I was thinking to myself 'Fair enough, why don't you give that to the bloody patient too because if he could tolerate me he wouldn't have copped it.'

Anyway, that was alright, I finally passed my exam. I'd been a good girl up until then and I got called into her office. I had to stand on the mat and get the same old lecture. As I began to walk out through the door she said, 'Come back here' and I went back and stood on the mat and a grin comes on her face, 'You owe me another mat, you've worn a hole in that one.' 'Oh, what colour would you like matron?' and fled.

Both of the matrons, the mid one and the other one. They used to follow me around. They used to come and camp with me down at Point McLeay. They'd stay in bed and do my cleaning for the day. I'd say 'If only I could remember that lecture on tolerance.' She'd say 'Don't say you've forgotten it, you heard it every day of the year for two years.'

Anything to do with book work was hard. Anything to do with sitting and studying was hard because I just wanted to be out there and going. I sat there for all that bloomin' time, the lecturers used to come and wake me up and say 'You'd better wake up, you're wanted on the phone' and I had no interest whatever in it. I only went into it because it was a fight to start off with. I never really had my heart in it. Something must have seeped in. So I thought go out by yourself and try your luck. I learned more out there because when you're doing your midwifery, you're only allowed to have twenty deliveries and you're fighting the medical students and everyone else because they've got to get their quota of deliveries in. When you go out there by yourself, well, by gee you do it. I used to have my book propped up there and 'Don't push' turn the page 'Push.' Here it is in my kitchen now, I see it every day and I laugh.

With my cricket career, I only played two games before I was in the state team and one game there and I was in the Australian team but that was all flash in the pan, it was good. The reporters used to come around and they'd want to interview the 'native nurse', we were natives in those days. Of course the captain and vice-captain and the managers, they were the big shots, they wanted to be in the news so they put the kobosh on that, which was good anyway, because I didn't know what to bloody well say.

I got a hat trick in my first game. I've still got the ball. I was a fast bowler but you see being a blackfella, I conserved energy, didn't I and they'd never seen me bowl before and I'd only take about four steps and I'd take it off my shoulder. They'd have their bat up and they'd be gone. They were expecting slow balls. It was surprise.

Out here in Quorn as kids, we used to play with a stick and stone. The old mayor here would tell you I had a mean throw. We'd have competitions on the way home from school and the blokes in the pub would stand and watch us and they'd put their money on me because there would be me and the boys. You know those cups on the top of electric light poles? We used to shy them. The town was in darkness all the time. We didn't know we were doing that much damage because we only had hurricane lamps out at the home, like tilley lights.

I'd pick a ball up at the 'Gabba' and put it on the middle stump. I've got a scrap book there. Just put it on the middle stump there, no hassles. I couldn't throw it now because my shoulder's out now. I could throw a stone at my dog. I'd miss the dog but I'd stand there with my shoulder in agony. I enjoyed my sport, very much so and I still love it. I get out there and play golf with my blackfella flag stuck on my bag. Even now when I go to Port Augusta, this bloke calls out the names and the girls laugh. He calls 'Faith, Mrs F Thomas,' and there's a pause, 'that dark lady' and of course, everyone now, now that they've got to know me, they wait for it then all the lips go 'Lady!' and then Grossy will sing out, 'Shit that must be you Snow White.' I was the only Aboriginal woman playing golf in Port Augusta, but I've got Elsie Jackson going now.

I won the NADOC Sportswoman of the Year (Senior) last year. Charlie Jackson's daughter won the Junior. There were a lot of applications too, I got a real surprise, but the girls from here wrote a letter.

One thing I feel denied is that I didn't learn my language and the Dreaming stories. I can't speak my own language and God, I've tried. I tried to talk Pitjantjatjara at the University. I was the only blackfella there and I was the only one who failed. I shamed us. I just don't have a thing for language. I know when I started this patrol up here, they'd all say to me 'Naanga' and I'd say, 'Oh you're a black bastard yourself' and eventually after about three months, my old aunties couldn't handle it any longer. 'You'll come down for tea tonight my girl.' And down I went, Aunty Alice and Aunty Annie. They sat me down and said 'We're going to teach you to talk your own language. When we say *naanga* to you,

we're saying to you *goodday* and you say to us *wandu*
you're *alright*. So I know that now. (Nunga around
Adelaide means 'Aboriginal person.')

Then they'd chat to me and rattle off their language.
That's how they were going to teach me. Anyone who
tries to teach me, I get in so much strife, it's not funny.
We had a language out there at Colebrook that only
Colebrooks know and it was because of these kids who
came in and couldn't speak English, they say something
and the kids would say, that means so and so. So there's
a Colebrook language that's all mixed up. This is what I
found hard when I went to do the Pitjantjatjara course,
that I was going to have to uneducate myself before I
even started. Some of the things we used to say were
probably quite dirty. We weren't allowed to mention
Aboriginal or talk lingo or anything like that. If we said
'Shut up' it was swearing. It was strict but then it had to
be with all those kids. You couldn't just let them all
loose.

I didn't get to travel overseas with my cricket because
I was nine months through my mid (midwifery) which I
hated and I was so far behind anyhow because that was
the year I was choofing around with the Australian
team. If I toured I would have had to start all over
again. Now that's another thing that I regret, that
I didn't go, in hindsight now. I should've because I
could've come back and done that year. It was my one
and only opportunity to go to England.

In Australia we played against England and New
Zealand. It was just like an ordinary Saturday afternoon
game of cricket. By then old Victor Richardson and
Howard Mutton, they decided that I had to have a run
up. They said 'You're going to do your cartilages in' and
'you're off balance' and things like that. 'You point your
foot when the ball's going there.' They used to try and
make me change my style, so I used to take about ten
steps run up, but nevertheless I did my cartilages in.
The other two girls in the team were both doctors, Barb
Orchard and Ruth Dow, she was the one that got me
into hockey, Ruth Dow. I played for varsity. I had to
take this run up and there'd be this bickering amongst

the Australian team and I used to wander off and do my own thing. When you bowl, you're supposed to put your foot where the ball's going but blackfella comes in like this and takes the weight across but I could hook them down.

Have you ever seen a stump go over a wicket keeper's head? Let me show you something, I can brag about this. (Faith produces a press clipping). The stump went over her head and she caught the bail. *England captain Mary Duggan was clean bowled by Faith Coulthard.* That was up at the 'Gabba'. I had all Joyce Hobbs' cricket gear. People would just lend you bats and things because you really had nothing. Charlie Perkins, when he went to England with the soccer team, he was too frightened to take his coat off because he had one sleeve missing out of his shirt. We formed the Aboriginal Sports Foundation to help the up and coming sports kids who had nothing. Let them enjoy their sport without hassles, like we had. Not that I had any hassles. I couldn't have cared less whether we had shoes or not.

My son doesn't play cricket. I'm teaching him golf now. All he can remember is 'Put your head down or we'll knock it off' when he was in the bassinet. I'd be out at the cricket with this bassinet with a kid in it. 'Hang on a minute' I'd be saying because I'd be breast feeding him and I'd run back onto the field. The best scores I ever made was when I was eight months pregnant. I was still playing see. I was hopeless with a bat, a real slasher but they used to literally underarm the ball to me and I'd stand there all protruding and I'd make the runs then.

Getting back to my people now, diabetes and heart are the problems for the Adnyamathanha people. They're just dropping dead from the heart. Diabetes is more or less a hereditary thing but it can be controlled. I think I'd be the only Coulthard that hasn't got it. I keep getting myself checked out. I've had it on occasions when I've been under stress, then it'll show its ugly head. I just thought I'll get out of stressful situations.

When I was nursing, one thing that always worried me was that women at Point Pearce, Point McLeay, would always come to me and ask how they could stop having babies. They'd send away for things. It was one thing that never came into the nursing programme. I can remember one woman come to me with a disk (perhaps a diaphragm?) and while I was trying to nut it out she got pregnant so I always felt a bit guilty about that. It was a queer thing that she sent away for. I didn't know anything about ovulation anyhow because in those days no-one really talked about it. Different ones were coming up and asking and their health was going down and they were dying and leaving mobs of kids behind and they were terribly anaemic. I thought, 'What about family planning? Let's go for quality, not quantity. How am I going to do this?'

This family planning clinic started in the Adelaide Hospital and I thought I'll go down and have a chat with this old dear. They thought it was a great idea because they had no Aboriginal girls who used to go to their clinic. I thought you can't do anything unless you're in an organisation and can get some backing. We got some money but I got opposition from people like Charlie Perkins who said it was genocide. I said 'Right Charles, look at you for instance, you've got three kids, all beautifully spaced. Now why? Because you've got the know how. Why can't we give that know how to other people?' 'No, it's still racial genocide.' I said 'It's racial genocide when a woman's pregnant every bloody year and she dies and what happens to her eight or nine kids?' I said 'Something has to be done about that.' I believed in what I was doing. They all threw the flak at me and I just kept on going.

I spent two years doing it in Adelaide and ended up with the title of 'Sister Yellow Raincoat.' The younger ones would say 'Here comes Sister Yellow Raincoat.' I'd say 'Have your fun but wear your yellow raincoat.' I had to get myself something that we could laugh about. I'd sit for hours with those kids around Adelaide and with women too.

When I worked at Point McLeay and Point Pearce, no-one ever said thanks but I got a lot of thanks out of this. I got a lot of satisfaction.

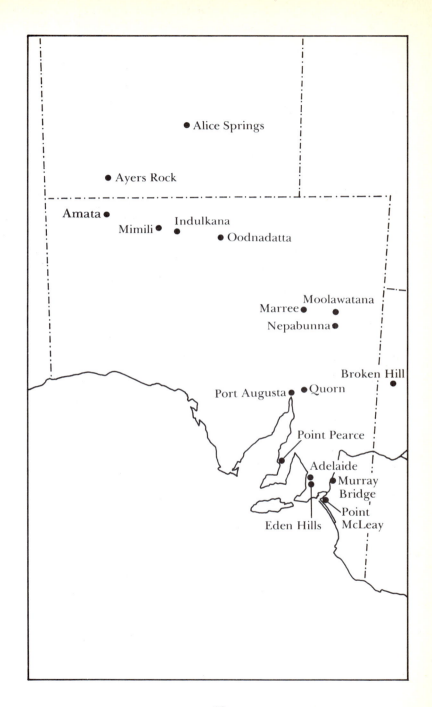

● Alice Springs

● Ayers Rock

Amata ●

Mimili ●   Indulkana ●

● Oodnadatta

Moolawatana

Marree ●   ●

Nepabunna ●

Broken Hill

Port Augusta ● ● Quorn   ●

Point Pearce
●

Adelaide
● ● Murray
    Bridge
    ● Point
Eden Hills   McLeay

I can honestly say that there was only one bloke at Point Pearce who said thanks to me and that was Oscar Kartinyeri. He came one night at nine o'clock and said thank you very much for putting me off the grog. He begged for ages. I had said to him, 'I'll give you these tablets mate and if you drink I'll kill you.' He said after, 'My kids had a beautiful Christmas. The best Christmas they ever had. Thank you.'

I think they thought I was their lackey. I used to walk those streets at Point McLeay with a bloody big oxygen cylinder over my back. It was all night, every night.

I found that family planning was one of the most important parts of my nursing. It was what I got most satisfaction out of and it was probably because I got so much opposition. I like a fight. I could feel the appreciation from the women too because they were just so desperate. 'Bloody pregnant again and I've still got the other one in nappies.' Post natal depression is recognized now but in those days no-one knew what it was and you'd see mothers shaking the hell out of their kids. That's what it was but it never had a handle.

When I was in the north-west on patrol at Ernabella, a mother was trying to suffocate her baby. That baby is a girl of twenty now. The mothers had a choice when I was on patrol — Oodnadatta, Amata or a bush birth and this one said she wanted a bush birth and I happened to be at Indulkana. We had an old tin shed there with the stores in it. The men ran in. They'd come thirteen miles to get me. That little baby was on the way out. We unchoked her and took her on patrol with us. We made her little dresses out of flour bags and a thing to keep the flies off her. I got really interested in that kid.

When I went back up to Ayers Rock for the handover I got out of the car and the people come over and grabbed my hand and said 'Come and see your girl. She's got a headband now, she's got a boyfriend now.' They're so proud of that kid, but it's my kid. Her name's Hilda. I remember going through this book of 2,000 girls' names and the only name that wasn't in the bloody book was Hilda. So Hilda it is.

Getting back to the mission days again. I think the

missionaries were marvellous people. I've got nothing against them anyhow. I was lucky, I had three mums.

I'll show you this quote from a book I dug up. It's got a quote from the Quorn Local Board of Health from the old Colebrook Home days. 'These children have at the best the mental capacity of at least three years below that of white children and consequently are placed in classes . . . with children much younger than them and as they arrive at sexual maturity at a very early age, they become a definite menace morally when associated with younger white children. When they remain here in idleness they become an added menace . . .'

Eventually, in my dotage, I'm going to write all this up as a history of Colebrook Home but in the meantime, I'm too busy playing golf and doing things like that while I can.

ADC (Aboriginal Development Commission) have purchased Colebrook Home and I've just sent my submission to DAA (Department of Aboriginal Affairs) for some funding. There's Lois (O'Donoghue), Stuart, my son, and myself on the committee from Quorn, then there's Yvonne, Des and George Tongerie. Eventually, I'll flog this house and we're planning to get units out there. The first priority is to paint the joint and put floor coverings in and that will be the cultural centre to show the history and all the stuff that I've collected over the years, like this book. Sister Hyde left all the old lantern slides and every time we put them in a projector to show them, they crack, they're so damn brittle, so eventually they came across a process to take them off so that cost me about $2,500. I've stuck everything else in Mortlock Library and kept copies for myself but in case anything happened to me, Mortlock's got it. (Mortlock Library in the State Library of South Australia).

Once we get out there, we'll sit and talk about what we want done but there'll be a caravan park for visitors and we'll chuck in an ablution block there and then we'll put some units up for those who want them. They'll be for anyone connected with Colebrook. We've got two young kids out there now, my grandchildren (Aboriginal way). My old mate up the road gave me a double bed to put out there. Maud and George (Tongerie) were the first two in it and now these two kids so it's great and the creek's running. It's fantastic.

Audrey Kinnear

Audrey is Lorna's younger sister but has lived an entirely different life. When quite young, Audrey was placed in the Koonibba Children's Home and later attended college in Adelaide and qualified as a nurse. After she married and had children, she, like many others in similar situations, traced her family connections. This has been very stressful for her, especially as her mother went missing some years ago and has never since been found. Audrey and Lorna now spend a lot of time together helping each other in their different ways. Audrey is working in an alcohol and drug rehabilitation programme in Port Augusta.

Finding Family

In the children's home at Koonibba (near Ceduna on the west coast of South Australia) we were like a big family because most of us were related. The ones that I've associated more with, were my cousins, Colleen and Rosie Tchuna and Joycey Barton. The four of us and Daphne used to get around a lot together, Daphne left the home then and went off to Mt Margaret in Western Australia to work but we used to muck around a lot together. Diana Prayta was another one, she was a relation.

In the children's home, we had a time when the older girls used to look after a younger one and they'd do things like washing your hair and things like that. They were like our mothers, I suppose, making sure we were dressed properly. We had happy times.

In those days we didn't have television, we used to tell a lot of stories in the sand and we used to go out looking for any bits of broken china or pretty glass and tell stories with the pretty glass. If you got a piece with a nice pattern on it, it might have been the skirt of a dress or something like that. We used to spend hours doing that sort of thing. Then we had our duties to do too before we went to school, like milking the cows and separating the cream from the milk, I used to quite like doing that. Bringing the wood in and that sort of thing, mainly the boys did that. Saturdays was a big clean up where you scrubbed the floors and tables and the seats, the forms we used to call them, in the dining room. Other happy times were days when we went for trips to Denial Bay. One of the things that I remember was when we got out of the truck and came over the sand-hills. You could see the beautiful ocean, the open sea, we'd all run down there with excitement.

Another thing I remember enjoying was the bush walk which was part of nature study at school. We walked miles sometimes looking at blossoms and different plants in the bush. The other thing that sticks in my head is going up to the rock hole. There was always water there and it was a place where you could meditate, although we didn't have that word in our language. I suppose it's a place where you went and thought a lot and looked around. I can remember looking across the horizon and thinking that must be where Mt Margaret way is. We knew it was west somewhere but had no idea really where the railway line went and things like that. So those were the nice things.

There was discipline too as there is in any institution. I can remember a couple of times Hans Gaden who was the farm manager at the time coming over to discipline a couple of boys who were naughty. We used to pinch raw onions, we ate onions with salt on them! They had this shed where they used to store the onions and they were mainly brown onions. We used to go in there and sneak some out and put salt on them and Joycey will tell you that too because she was part of our group that used to do that. It used to be lovely. And we'd go wild peach hunting and bird nesting when it was time so you kept pretty busy.

Then the other very important occasion in our life was the Sunday, because it was church day. The church was the centre of the community. It was when we all came together. There was a real excitement in the air when you put your Sunday best on, we'd march to church and sing our heads off. Christmas Eve was always special because of the church service and hymn singing and then big boxes used to come from the different Lutheran congregations throughout the state and we knew the presents were all there and we used to go to church and come home and we used to get our new dresses and things like that, which was nice at the time.

So my memories of the home were, on the whole, happy times and if there was a negative side I suppose it was that we really weren't prepared for the outside world. Some of us showed a bit of potential at school and they sent us off for further education at Concordia College. I left the home and this is what a lot of people don't appreciate, I left the children's home on my own and I was the first Aboriginal girl that was sent to Concordia and it wasn't easy. I cried a lot to myself at night, because it was lonely. I'd left my family of all the other kids in the home and I wasn't at college long when I realised that I may never go back to that again because I'd gone forward and life's different then. So there was conflict there.

I went back for one holiday. We used to have iron beds with those black and white covered mattresses and all you had was a tin locker by your bed. It was quite spartan. At that time, your lifestyle there and what was being offered to you at college was different and I can remember feeling a bit strange going back and not really being happy about it. So the next holiday I stayed with a family at Ceduna, Staninowskis, Olive and Pat. Colleen was with them too then.

We stayed at Colona one school holiday. We preferred to stay in a family home rather than going back to the mission. Colleen had started at Concordia then. Pat Kleinig was managing Colona then and Joycey, Rosie and myself were on holiday. That's when I nearly drowned in the tank. I have never got out of my depth in the water since.

Concordia was good in that we were all christian kids, all Lutherans and so everybody tried hard to make you feel at home when it came to school holidays. I used to get invited back to some of the girls' homes for the holidays. I can remember staying with Coral Chirmer who was in my class and staying with her family at Cambrai and her place overlooked a river or creek and that was nice. So I suppose that it helped. They couldn't throw you out in the street in the holidays because you had nobody.

There are so many things that have happened in my life I don't know how I've survived.

I kept pretty well up with the school work. The kids from Concordia came from all over Australia and you'd sit with a group and have two hours study every night after tea in the dining room. You'd all get your chairs and study, then you'd have your supper and go to bed.

50

If you were struggling with something, there was always help. We used to walk crocodile style to Concordia because the girls' hostel was in Wattle Street and Concordia was two blocks away. We were always in uniform of course. We used to put our pleated tunics under the mattress at night to press them and I think that was a common thing that happened at boarding school.

One of the traumatic experiences at Concordia was when we were learning Aboriginal history in relation to Tasmania and they were talking about the Aboriginals there, being herded up and being shot and I broke down and cried and cried and cried and nobody could understand. When I went to one of the families on holidays, I can remember the daughter asking me why I cried. I sort of explained a bit to her but whether she understood what I was going through I don't know. I suppose many, many children who went to schools similar to Concordia experienced the same thing, people not being sensitive to the fact that that was part of your heritage.

My brother Harold was in the children's home at the time and we were close and we used to write. He's next in age to me and he never married. When he left the home he lived over on a farmer's place at Blyth but he stayed with me recently after being in the Royal Adelaide Hospital. He went on from the children's home to Blyth and worked for the Henschke's farm there. When the kids got old enough to leave, they were placed with families on farms. I went to Blyth a couple of times when I was at college to stay with him and went to the pictures and things like that. They included him as a part of their family and he had a long association with them. When I went back to the Concordia Jubilee, two of the Henschke girls were there and they were talking about Harold in terms of endearment, so he had become part of their extended family too. He lived and worked there and they looked after him and then he went back to the west coast and he's worked a lot for the farmers over there. He used to do reaping and things like that. When I went over there as a member of the Outback Areas Trust, the women were so pleased to

51

meet the sister of Harold because everybody knew him over there and he's always got a bed with farmers there. He lives mainly in Penong now.

When I was at Concordia my sister Lorna (whose story follows this) was already a mother and I don't know whether she had her tribal husband then, but she certainly had her first daughter, Gloria. I didn't see much of her because she was in Fowlers Bay and Yalata. She's next in line to Mabel, then there's Harold and me.

After Concordia, I started nursing at Osmond Terrace. I applied and was interviewed and accepted there. I did two years there which was quite good because it was something I wanted to do from my early life at Koonibba, watching the sisters in the hospital there, weighing the babies and all that. I thought I'd love to be a nurse. I dreamed then of course, that one day I'd go back and work with my people but somewhere along the track you change direction. There are so many other things that influence your life.

Osmond Terrace was small, it was a private hospital and I had a couple of really good friends there, we used to get around together, we used to go to the coffee shop together after work on Norwood Parade. One of the things that I can remember being disturbed by was the electric shock treatments there. Before the treatment the patient would know you, next thing after the treatment they'd sort of look at you and say 'Who are you?' Being so young, you didn't connect the two, until later.

I was the only Aboriginal nurse there at Osmond Terrace. I can remember enjoying working in the theatre and there was blood everywhere from surgery. Interestingly enough, since I've been with Drug and Alcohol Rehabilitation Service, I went to Osmond Terrace just before they finished renovating it all and I was able to go and look at the rooms that we slept in, which now seem very small and I sat in the little garden area where there was a little fish pond. I went up to the room in the back block where they have now got the methadone treatment and actually walked into the room that I slept in, so that was good because it's all changed now with the renovations. Osmond Terrace

52

now is called Warinilla which is the drug rehabilitation place.

I was there two years then I transferred to the Royal Adelaide Hospital. Communal living there was good because if you've been plucked out from somewhere which is miles away and have nowhere to go, and actually live-in there, it was very good. It provided us with a home and on the spot job. That was hard too in a sense because we worked from 6.30 in the morning and we had a break in the afternoon and went back and worked until 10.30. They were your shifts. Things were very, very strict in those days and we had study in our time off. One day you finished at 3.30 before your day off and you were supposed to have attended lectures and studied in that time.

It was very discipline oriented. You didn't dare sit on beds. Beds were very, very well made before the honorary surgeons and medical people came with their team of students. Lois O'Donoghue (now well known in Aboriginal Affairs and Australian of the Year in 1988) was already a Charge Nurse there on the surgical wards. We had the old people's wards as well. I can remember laying out bodies in the old wards and one that was fly-blown!

One of the things I remember was being rostered to lay out bodies when there were deaths during the night. One funny occasion was when medical students played a game on the orderly who used to wheel the bodies to the morgue. A student was covered with sheets and halfway down to the morgue, which was on a slope, the body sat up in the dark. The poor orderly let the brouche go, he was so frightened.

The only Aboriginal patient I can remember is one from Darwin who had the bends. He was an uncle of Mary Anne Bin-Sallik (who recently gained a PhD from Harvard) She can remember me nursing him and taking him out in the wheelchair in the sun. She told me that a few years later. I used to do things then like go out to the Millswood Hostel and visit the young girls there on my days off. We were always searching out the Nungas. We used to go out and watch Charlie and

Johnny play soccer out at the Hindmarsh Oval. Charlie Perkins, John Moriarty and Gordon Briscoe.

And there was a lady, a Mrs Christie at Croydon. Her home was always open to Aboriginal people. We used to spend a lot of our days off with her, and at the Winterlich's home too. They really opened up their home to me. I've had a long association with them and I consider them family too. They really helped me cope better with city life. They were involved in the church at Koonibba too. They used to live at Parkside where Concordia was and when they moved to Myrtle Bank we used to still call in.

I was there two years. I didn't finish, I missed out on one of my final subjects which I completed when I came to Port Augusta. At that stage I went through feelings — so many things — it's hard to explain, so many things going on in my life. I was determined I was going to make it. One of the things I can remember is sitting on my bed and facing the mirror every morning saying to myself you are going to get there. At that time the whole environment was negative to Aboriginal people. Peoples' attitudes were prejudiced and racist. I can remember reading one article which said an adult Aboriginal had the intellectual mind of a 10 year old or 5 year old or something like that.

I remember thinking to myself, 'you are going to prove this wrong', so I worked really hard and really psyched myself up. At the Royal Adelaide, I think Lois has made the statement that you always had to do what you were told, you really had to polish your shoes, just about see yourself in them, always had to be tidy and all that because you were not only proving that you could do it, but you were also paving the way for other Aboriginal people to follow and it was always on your mind.

I did a bit of nursing out in an old folks' home at Fullarton and it was while I was there they asked me to enter the Miss Australia Quest. One of the things that made up my mind was that night there was a film on television about the struggles about the blacks in America. It was another chance to open the doors for Aborigi-

Audrey Kinnear in the Miss Australia quest, third from the right.

55

nal people. It was a bit of a struggle having to go to parades and things like that but I quite enjoyed it, although I didn't really have the support behind me to do it. I forget who it was now, who paid for my dress and eventually I paid him back because I couldn't afford it. I was only on nurses' wages, I couldn't afford to buy the outfits to be in the parade. I did hire one, when some of the entrants were presented at the interval at the circus at West Parklands. I remember John Moriarty and other Nungas came to a fashion parade fundraiser at Centennial Hall. There was quite a group anyway that came. So there was a little bit of support.

After that I came to Port Augusta to work at the hospital. I came because there was always that thing in my mind to get back and I saw Port Augusta as one of the areas where I could come into contact with my family again.

I was about 24 then. I wrote to Port Augusta and was accepted and when I came up here, the new conflicts started. I got on well with the nurses in the home but the hospital didn't allow the Aboriginal women to be admitted to the General Ward. They had a sleep-out. I was in the ward with another nurse and I can remember picking up the thermometer tray and heading out from the General Ward to the sleep-out and she said 'Audrey you can't do that!' They had separate thermometer trays. Everything was separate. The winter used to be so freezing out there too. I suppose, thinking about it, some of it was for reasons of hygiene but it created a bit of upset for me. Outpatients was another area where Aboriginal people had to wait outside to be attended to. But I wasn't strong enough then myself to make any changes. The Children's Ward was another upsetting place because there were Aboriginal kids dying of gastro. You could see them breathing their little lives away. You knew that if the kid came in from Davenport, they'd be very lucky to live. Those were traumatic things.

Then I met Laurie, got married, started to have a family and all the time the conflict was within me. I knew that I had to make contact with my mother some-

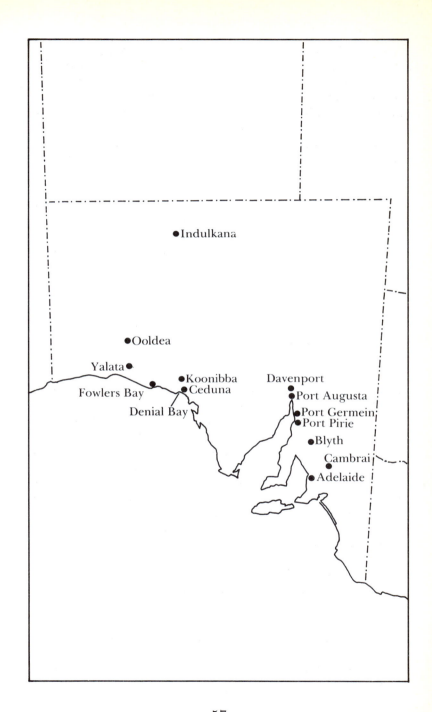

Indulkana

Ooldea

Yalata

Fowlers Bay

Koonibba
Ceduna

Denial Bay

Davenport
Port Augusta
Port Germein
Port Pirie
Blyth
Cambrai
Adelaide

time and I can remember Mrs Mac (Williams) coming up to the hospital from the mission saying to me 'Your mother's out there' but it took a long time because emotionally I wasn't ready. Later I was working at the surgery for Dr Byron Sadler, who was a caring person, the first time that I saw people being treated all the same. Some people who came in from Davenport, their hygiene wasn't too good but Byron never flinched and treated people as if there was nothing different about them. He was a lovely person, a christian man of course, and he said to me one day, 'Audrey your mum is in hospital' and I went through great stress — I knew I should visit her but I just couldn't get myself to do it. I felt helpless and psychologically confused.

Anyway, eventually we did make contact. Laurie was the first that went out because I was just about a psychiatric case at that stage, torn between what I should do and whether I should make contact. I wanted to and yet I couldn't so he said, 'I'm going out there and I'll find out how your mum is,' and he found her. She said, 'Tell Audrey I'm alright and when she's ready, she can see me.' Lorna was there too, because mum was living with Lorna at the time at Davenport. They were in one of those houses just by the shop there and so eventually I did get to see her. Laurie made it easier. I went out to see her there.

In one sense, I went through a lot of guilt feelings and all that for taking so long but when I really examined the whole thing again, I just feel I couldn't have done it any earlier as I was pretty fragile at that time, emotionally. I started to take her for outings. One of the last things I did for her was take her to the surgery, she had an ulcer on her leg that wasn't healing. I took her to Byron and he dressed it. Laurie and I were just thinking about having her stay with us. We used to have a room at the back. We thought mum might like to be independent and we were moving towards having her home, but at that time I'd taken up a job in the Public Health Department in Aboriginal Health and part of that was going in the Welfare car with the *tea and sugar train* on the Transcontinental line.

Prior to me going on one of those trips Lorna's tribal husband, who was an old man, had had a heart attack and I was working at Davenport at the time as a Community Health Nurse, and I was able to ring the ambulance and get him to hospital. He died and it was during that period that Mabel our sister from Port Pirie decided that she'd better take mum for a while to give Lorna a break. After that was all organised, I went off in the Welfare car and whilst I was away, mum disappeared from near a roadhouse at Port Pirie.

Mabel came to Davenport thinking that mum would be there and got such a shock when she wasn't. It came out at the inquest. Mabel was the last to see her. The police had Mabel locked up that night. She had been walking with mum all day in Pirie and they decided they'd go out to the roadhouse to get a lift back to Port Augusta but because she went in the roadhouse with a bottle of beer in her hand, I think the girl got a bit nervous and rang the police and she was locked up for the night. That's when mum was left there, the police didn't know the old lady was with Mabel and she hasn't been seen since. The last sighting was by the petrol attendant who saw her walking away from the roadhouse there. I think a truckie might have spotted her later, walking from the roadhouse towards Port Germein. That was the last sighting.

Our cousin Joycey and Mabel went to the Police Station at Port Pirie and reported it. The records show no follow-up. They went to the Welfare and they couldn't get any help from there. They went to the Council at Davenport, they went everywhere. Uncle Jimmy (James) came and he was one of the searchers and trackers and people went out there on their own. Prior to that, the other relatives had made reports but there was no follow up. In the meantime, I'd returned from my trip, working on the train. A sad thing about it is the police didn't realise that there was another daughter, that was me, and they hadn't got in contact with me. Action was then taken but six days had already passed. Lorna wasn't that comfortable with Laurie at that stage, like she is now. They get on really well but back then she didn't know him that well. She didn't call on him and so he wasn't aware mum was missing until I came back. She waited until I came back then we turned everything upside down, went down to the Police Station and since then we had the Superintendent of Police ringing me at home and giving me reports but this was about 5 or 6 days later. There was a Sergeant Roberts at the Port Pirie Police Station who was very good.

We had the inquest about 12 months later and I wrote a letter to the Coroner because months had gone by and I asked reasons for the delay. It was because he'd written to the communities wherever he thought mum might have been, even Broken Hill. All the communities were investigated and they were satisfied that nobody had seen her. I've got a copy of the Coroner's Report. Some hurtful things came out I suppose. One was that Mabel had walked mum around Pirie nearly all day because Clem (her husband) was drinking. When Mabel went back home next morning after she was let out of the cells, she got the shock of her life when she couldn't find mum. She came into Davenport thinking that's where mum would've been. There was tension and ill feeling because Lorna then started thinking of Mabel neglecting mum. A few months later, I had a job in Port Pirie and took Lorna for a drive in the area to get the two sisters together again.

Laurie and I had to organise the inquest, the last sitting was in Adelaide because at the first hearing in Port Augusta, I just felt as if the wool was being pulled over our eyes. The officer in charge up there, of the Pirie Police didn't attend the first hearing and the reason they gave was that he was on annual leave. I can remember saying 'I'm not satisfied with that, I'd like him to be called.'

I could see at the second hearing, although I was very upset, why he wasn't called. It was because he more or less just thought mum was an old lady and that she was deranged, and the telex that he sent over to Ceduna was that she was a 'deranged old Aboriginal woman.' We had Pat Mudge to represent us who was really good. She gave up her other engagements to do that.

When we went to Adelaide, Andrew Collett took it on, he asked questions like, 'Why wasn't there a dog search?', 'Why wasn't there an aerial search?' and the guy that was in charge of the Pirie Police Station just said he didn't think it was necessary. But Sergeant Roberts was really good, during the inquest at Port Augusta he came over and he shook our hands and he said, 'Mrs Kinnear if that was my mother, I'd be holding an enquiry too.' He was really nice. I spoke to him a couple of times when we first went to the Pirie Police Station. So the poor old dear has never been found and I was only thinking the other day that if she's still in this area, where her remains are, it's off her homelands and if her remains could be found, we could take them back and bury them on her homelands where her spirit could rest.

But there's just been nothing, just been absolutely nothing. I had to see a psychiatrist and one of the things he did stress was I should continue working. I don't know how I continued working, because I also had a counselling and support role with the other members of the family. We had a couple of instances a few years after, when my brother-in-law was saying silly things when he got drunk like he'd hit her on the head and that was very distressing. I had to play the counsellor again and get everybody back on an even keel. It took Lorna a long time to get over it, because she was the one who cared for mum and she often used to cry and talk about it with me and sometimes when we sit outside she still talks about everything. Sometimes I wonder how we recovered from that. I think some of us must be very strong people to be plucked from where we were, the lifestyle that we had and to come through it all, reasonable unscathed. I say reasonable unscathed because a lot of the trauma people can't see. You put on this mask of coping, you have to otherwise you'd go under.

It's a sad thing not knowing your relatives. If you don't grow up with your family, you miss out on all those years. The other very real conflict I had was in relation to my own children, whether I should encourage them to learn their Aboriginality but society being

61

what it is, we decided that we'd give our kids survival skills. One was to give them good education, the other was to help them to make their own decisions, which they've done very well at. I am noticing that Lisa, particularly since she's been in Darwin working, she's getting interested in Aboriginal people. She went to Jabiru and talked to the old fellas that came in and things like that. I think that's something that they'll pursue if they want to.

We gave them the skills to survive but I wasn't sure how much I should take them back to where my life was and all that. They understand what we went through because they were part of the period when mum was missing, they often used to see me break down and cry and go through depression. Laurie was really the strength that kept us all together and he's been a wonderful support to Lorna, I mean she thinks the world of him.

When the little fella, (Lorna's grandson) was killed in 1986 at the age of 5, Lorna fortunately had our telephone number. It always used to amaze us how she remembered it, she must have had it down on a piece of paper. She's never had a formal education and can't read or write. He was hit by a car on Carlton Parade and she was at the shop and the dog came running back. The dog was always with him and she knew straight away that there was something wrong. She saw the people there and she saw the ambulance and she rang us straight away.

We were living in the hills then, quite a distance from Port Augusta. We had the advantage however of knowing professional people and the system. Laurie got on the phone straight away to the hospital and spoke to one of the sisters in Outpatients. She said, 'Come in straight away, it's critical.' I found myself in a dilemma as a professional person, knowing that little Lawrence had brain death because I saw him in theatre in Outpatients. The doctor on duty advised me that in consultation with the doctor in Adelaide, he makes a decision about whether to send a retrieval team in. The decision was then made that the retrieval team wouldn't be coming up. I knew there was little hope. At the same time I had Lorna and Thelma with me and I had to then make them feel that there was hope. I was in this bind. I was Lawrence's aunty.

We noticed the night that it happened that Lorna had gone back to her tribal ways, she was walking along the street and she was singing and wailing and she was quite oblivious to us even being there. We let her go through that before we took her to the hospital. You're going to have me crying now.

It was really sad to see her go through that and then going up to the hospital. The next day in Intensive Care, Joycey walked in and said to Laurie and I, 'Little fella's been dead for a long time.' She rang up Uncle Jimmy James from Intensive Care, and he came straight away. Aunty Myra, came from Indulkana. I suppose one of the really positive things about Aboriginal people is when there's tragedy and death or something, everybody rallies around. I thought I'd emphasise the dilemma that one's in knowing that there's no hope and yet making the others feel that there is hope. As a nurse, I knew that the life support was only on for a couple of hours.

When we got back to Lorna's the police were there and everybody else was really upset. They wanted someone to go back and identify the body, so they asked me. I had to do it. A couple of the staff that I know in Intensive Care were very concerned about me. They said, 'Are you up to doing this?', I did it. It was just a matter of going there and saying, 'Yes this is Lawrence Grantham.' We had a lovely letter from the Coroner because the enquiry showed that it was an accident. There wasn't alcohol or anything involved. He'd just run out on the road.

For weeks after, Lorna was ringing me up. She was so distressed because she couldn't understand, 'Why isn't the woman being punished that hit the boy?' I thought the only way I'm going to help her to overcome that was to make an appointment with the police. We went down there and the officer we spoke to was really nice and he sat down and explained to her.

I suppose the times we haven't had together have been sad because you never make up for those lost years of sharing and although the brothers and sisters all see each other I don't really know all my nieces and things like that because everyone's busy rearing their families. But there are times when we get together now. Lorna often talks about her life. I didn't fully understand how we came to be in the children's home but you never really make up for that time. There's always sadness there but I suppose with any of my family, Lorna's the one that's closest to me because we've shared a lot since then, things that have happened.

One day, now that the children have all grown up and are independent, once we settle back into Port Augusta I'd like to do a trip back with her, back in memory lane and go back to Ooldea, to our homeland. There are other places Lorna talks about when I was a baby like going to Coober Pedy before houses were there. Sometimes I don't know whether they're just dreams but over the years I feel as if I've been to Ooldea as a kid. There are some memories there but I don't know whether they're memories from other people talking about it. I think it's very, very important for my final *healing*, I suppose, of my inner spirit, to actually do the trip.

I don't know how old I was when I went into the children's home. When I became Chairperson of the Aboriginal Welfare Organisation, Aunty Myra was living at Indulkana but she grew up in the Riverland. She wrote to me and said, (I've got the letter somewhere) 'You are a sister to Mabel and Lorna. I saw you as a little kid playing at Ooldea.' One of the very important things that I must do, particularly with our own children, is to go and see things. Later on, if they want, they can get involved in Aboriginal Affairs, it's their choice.

Other hurtful things have been the conflicts that have occurred in Aboriginal Affairs. Like in 1984, I went to a conference, I think it was the first time for Aboriginal women, 100 Aboriginal women gathered in Canberra, and words like *coconuts* and being *whitewashed* were being said and it was very, very hurtful. So Aboriginal people can hurt each other very much too and not give

64

credit to those who have worked hard or have done things to help change the system. It's always easier, and I think this is very much so of the Australian society as a whole to knock the tall poppies, of putting people down rather than saying, 'This is great' because he or she has made it. Aboriginal people have done a lot of work towards changing attitudes or changing the government system for the better of Aboriginal people.

That still happens today and I think as a group Aboriginal people have to get together and work for the common good and support each other. It did hurt some of the women who were the leaders, the group leaders, at that conference, some of them really broke down afterwards because they thought it was being aimed at them. I found it very upsetting. It's hard to change anything with conflict all the time.

One of the very real problems I had was often being the first doing things and this has happened to Lois and others as well. At the time when you're offered things, you do it because if you knock it back then there might not be anything else offered, so you do it in the interests of the people as a whole. But because you're put on a pedestal or out there all the time, you lose some of yourself. You find that people call on you, which I don't mind, because if they see you as a person with skills or qualifications and the ability to give input into this area, you don't mind doing it, but it does put a lot of pressure on you.

It was very sad too to go back to see the children's home again at Koonibba and to find that it has been pulled down and there's just a plaque there.

The number of deaths amongst Aboriginal people has been terrible recently at Port Augusta. We've just had so many. People that you know and people that I grew up with in the children's home have been sitting in the parks abusing alcohol, to see them being homeless throughout and eventually dying, that all affects you.

White people don't understand why they drink and they think that I've been successful. They see the end product and see a person being in employment, being accepted in the community. Nursing has been wonderful for that because it's opened many doors. They see that but they don't understand the conflict inside you and it's difficult to be reassured unless it's with your very close friends. My family, of course, have experienced a lot of the trauma that I've gone through. Circumstances are often out of our control. I'm beginning to get inner peace and just accept that all this happened but it's very hurtful at the time.

NOTE: In December 1991, Lorna, Audrey and their sister Mabel, travelled back to Ooldea for the handing back of the Ooldea lands to the traditional Aboriginal owners, themselves included.

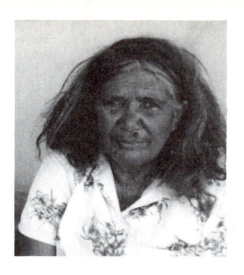

Lorna Grantham

Lorna's mother was a Pitjantjatjara/Yankuny-tjatjara woman and her father a European worker on the east-west railway near the edge of the Nullabor. Lorna grew up at Ooldea when Daisy Bates was living there. She later married her promised husband and together with others travelled from station to station doing casual work and living a semi-traditional life. Lorna is now a widow and grandmother and lives in Port Augusta. She still speaks her traditional language, as well as English.

Memories of Daisy Bates

I was born at Ooldea, when Daisy Bates was there. Daisy Bates stoppin' not far. Daisy Bates come around and saw me — mum told me. 'Oh! watjilyitja' — like that — she said watjilyitja — that's half-caste kids, watjilyitja. Instead of saying half-caste kids — say watjilyitja.

When I get little bit bigger, bigger, they was hiding me then. When I get big, we hide then under the big hollow tree. We always hide — me and Teddy and another girl. We go under the hollow tree when they try to send the half-caste kids away, we do trick. Was thinkin' about mum too — didn't want to leave her, and that other girl and Teddy. And they always make a big break, big break (windbreak) and we all sit down and play and they all sing out then and they put the blankets and dogs and we all hide under the blankets and they all sit down then and they put the dogs there on the top. Sittin' down there and they looking around everywhere — can't find 'em — we're under the blankets.

Police lady always trying to find half-caste kids, send them away to the home but I wouldn't leave mum. Once a month the police come — not all the time. They're walking. We got a camp a long way in the scrub and they come around and look around then — look around for half-caste kids then but not much people was there then — mission was nothing.

Daisy Bates was stopping at the top of the hill there with them — two tents — long dress and umbrella. After that, we get a little bit bigger. I was getting bigger and bigger and I was playing and playing and Daisy Bates — we was too frightened of Daisy Bates — all in white — shoes, socks white, dress white, umbrella white, hat white with netting on the top. Come around and we was under the bushes — Daisy Bates up there — up and down all the time.

'Daisy Bates' we singing out all the time — 'Daisy Bates'. Teasing. She was looking around everywhere — can't find us — we're under the trees hiding. Gets the police and all.

We're been there (at Ooldea) a long time and we been come to Tarcoola. Ooldea Mission was nothing then. We come to Tarcoola. We would stay in Tarcoola then. Long time staying there — policeman giving rations out then. We been come then — all in one — you know one tribes. My uncle was there, my auntie, mum's cousins, uncles — all them come to Tarcoola. We was sitting down there long time. Policeman telling us go and get water in the tank there. They did too — water and everything there. Ooldea Mission was nothing — (only) Daisy Bates was there. Come to Tarcoola.

After that we been sitting down, sitting down, sitting down, long time we been there. After that Martha was born then. Martha was born — sitting down there again and after that — long time we been staying there — after that Reggie been born then, Daisy's brother, youngest one — he was born then. We been sitting down, sitting down then and after that Edna William been born then too. Been there long time.

The policeman come around and tell them then they're going to put a mission at Ooldea and after that we went back, stay in Ooldea then.

Everyone getting run over by the train you know. Didn't understand what train is — lot of people been getting killed — broken leg, broken arm — do it on the train — jumping on train you know. Another lot there — told them about it — won't listen — they couldn't understand — get killed all the time — on the train. They jump on the trucks — not on the carriages — terrible thing.

That was before we was born, before when mum and them were young girls. They was sitting there making fire, cooking rabbits and all and after one man been come along and they can see the train. Standing there with the spear — see the train coming and they didn't know the train — see them run back then. When dad and mum come they was putting new railways up — young girl — long time.

Christmas time at school (building in background).
Lorna is second from left at the back.

Annie Lock, the missionary at Ooldea in 1934. Lorna's mother
May is to the right, probably holding baby Harold with Lorna
between Annie and May.

Went back to Ooldea when they put the mission up then. Miss Lock look after them for a bit. She the one who been staying there feeding the people when I was little and after them put a mission there and she was looking after mission. Daisy Bates been stopping there before no-one ever see them — never see the dark people, you know — didn't meet them — they come naked — no clothes on it — that's when Daisy Bates been meeting them.

Daisy Bates been coming around when I been laying down (baby). When I get bigger and bigger, Miss Lock take me then. Miss Lock would take me to Quorn. (To Colebrook Children's Home). I was staying there then. I was big then. Ruth McKenzie was big then. They was all big and who's that other one? Clara (Clara Coulthard). Miss Lock been take me, mum left me there at Ooldea, see. Never come back and pick me up. I was staying there long time. Left me there and go away then and I was sitting there thinking why doesn't she come down and why did she leave me here and I been thinking mum been going away west coast then. Audrey wasn't born, only Mabel, mum was taking Mabel from Ooldea to west coast. She been stopping around there and after there went back. Harold was baby then. My mum went back to Ooldea to see me but I wasn't there — I was here — Quorn.

Harold was still a baby when they came back and after that, sitting down, sitting down, sitting down — and everyone reckon 'No — Miss Lock been take 'em — Quorn — she'll bring 'em back.' After that, they put me on the train by myself, go back Ooldea — jump down — they been waiting for me to pick me up, take me to the mission. I was in (Ooldea) home then, sitting down in the home.

After that we been sitting down in the home, another lot came in then with no clothes on. One man was walking with the firestick with a lot of spears. Not proper naked, you know, something here (indicating pubic cover) and waddies. Can talk English, 'Give me tucker' 'Wanyu' (wait). We go inside and get a bag of clothes. Gave them two bag of clothes. Another lot was up on the hill there, waiting. Give them clothes and they put 'em on, put 'em on, they come this way then. Give them ration all out — long time ago.

Stay there a long time then, sitting down. Daisy Bates was there and after that, Daisy Bates shift into Wynbring. Won't stay then at Ooldea — old people follow Daisy Bates again to Wynbring, this side of Ooldea. There's Immarna, Barton, Mt Christie, Wynbring. There's a big stone there — big stone. We been playing there then, long time ago. We all put a green leaf and sit down all in a row and slide down. Big rock, still there. 'Ready, set, go'. We all playing down the hill — lot of fun.

After, they going in rockholes. We all been camping out. We go along — no water — rockhole's a long way. We put a camp in the middle and we sitting down there. 'Hey — no water.' Old people get a bucket, billy — cutting big roots under the tree — put leaves down and quick, stand sticks up, billy can full. That's how they make damper, tea and all. We had flour, sugar and water from the roots. Used to travel around long time ago. Men always come back with a kangaroo, little rabbits, always come back with that. No rifles in that time. Hunted with spears and woomeras.

Women get lot of seeds from the trees and when the wind come in they put them in that little shovel (wooden digging dish) and when the wind come they go like this then (winnowing) — clean them and after that they get a big stone, put 'em down, crush them up, clean them and after that they put water in them, mix them up and put the ashes on them — cook them. That's what they do, no flour. Sweet too — no sugar in it.

We got seeds off the tree and all sorts of different tuckers — quandong and that other tree — like a quandong only different again — not around here — like a peach only different, white inside but the skin's brown — bit brown. Walk along and feel hungry — just get them there and eat them — nice sweet one too. We learn from the old peoples. Songs, dancing too.

Another man again been gone (died). They dig a big hole you know when they gone and they tell 'em to go under the hole, put the sand all over and they go like this (indicating with hands) and you see them moving and they sing from there and you see that man come out from the hole then. Singing all night. That's what they do. Then mum and them was dancing. People was painted up. Mum was sitting down and big tree was there and uncle was standing there and I could see Daisy — put my head down there — another two half-caste kids there too. Daisy Bates always says watjilyitjas kids so I know. Put my head down. Keep out of her way.

We had songs when they feel happy, you know. Anything happen — when anyone die, they make a song, song about anyone been die, anything happen. And they cut their hair, cut all the hair off and roll it up.

We had to bury one fella. We girls were older than him. Make me sorry. We dig a hole because nobody wasn't there and only mum and another woman. No whitefellas there. Dig a big hole, cut all the feathers off the tree, like that tree there (bushy acacia tree). We was cutting them, cutting them, cutting them, put the leaves there in the hole — make them little bit warmer and they put like a bed and put a blanket underneath on the leaves and after that they tie this one (right arm) up with a little string, rag or something and leave this one (left arm). Put 'em in and put a lot of sticks on top — leave it open. Two years, nearly three years you leave it, come back to same thing there and cover over — bury it — like that — they go away then. Sit down about two or three years — you go back and cover that thing over. That's way they do it.

And this one here (dead body) they cut 'em (hair) and after that they make 'em tie hair up and wrap it around and around. Put red ochres on it and tie it around and around and around and around and they tell them you keep that and anybody when they have it under the pillow or anywhere — might be on the top, might be under the pillow you leave 'em. Anybody come around — pinch your tucker — it make them sick — nobody can't come around and pinch your tucker or blanket or anything like that. That's true! I can do that — no-one can go into my house. I've been having that thing too, you know.

When I was young girl we was all in that home there
and after when my old man finished and I been sitting
down thinking that when someone go in my house and
pinching my meat and sitting down eating it outside and
Isabel came around and (I) tell them 'Hey, what you
pinching the meat for?' and after that they tell me 'Oh,
come back, please.' They're sick! They said 'Lorna, feel
me, feel me' (healing massage) and I said 'No, no' 'Feel
me, feel me' and 'No'. I feel them then — make 'em
better again. 'Cos I've been having 'em long time but my
old man been keeping them away (her late husband's
spirit).

My old man (promised husband) was in that picture
on hill way to Quorn (probably the feature film *Kangaroo*) — he was in that picture too. My mother's uncle
there too and they was drinking that water like that —
kapi. He was standing with a woomera. You see him in
the film. Everyone was drinking out of the trough then.
The trough up there, windmill there. But another lot
been go there before but they all get money. My old
man speak up for the money. 'We come a long way to
make a picture. You make picture, you been taking
pictures, you'll have to give money out for everybody.'
Kangaroo was sitting down — scratching 'em (scratching himself under the arms). Man they doing 'em
(imitating). Oh! That's man's business. Woman not supposed to watch and the kangaroo's sitting down there
scratching. Man doing it, kangaroo doing it. But they
watching it in the picture now. Long time ago they not
allowed to see it.

We stayed at Wynbring a long time. Everybody been
cutting trees and selling them, lizard and all them
(artefacts). Long time ago. No pension was there then,
no pension, no social service, nothing. Cutting trees and
making things. And when they got the money, war been
start then (World War II). Train was up and down with
the soldiers. They having dinner Ooldea — soldiers.
Then they jump on the train and the cook give 'em out.
Every time, everyone, tea, bread, everything, they giving 'em out. Every time when that train stop there at
Ooldea. Wynbring, the same again, long time ago.

They always give money then, dark people there, always give money and from there asking for bread, tinned meat, everything, sugar. The cook drop all the bread then, dropping them when the train go along, they drop everything. Sugar, bag of sugar, they tie 'em up tight, with the string, tight, tea leaves, sugar, everything they all tie up, they drop 'em all the way and mum comes behind — I been running. She says get four loaves bread — all like that all the way — sugar, tea leaf for mum. Mum comes out. Everybody get money — leaving 'em out, everyone get money. That's how they been living there a long time.

Mum said, no social service, no pension. And they go out camping long way to the rockholes and after that I been going with them to another rock hole, not far from Malpuma and I been see emu tracks on the stone, (Dreaming story), seen the emu, all the little emus tracks gone hard on top of the rock.

Rockhole everywhere. One man been killed a big snake — big carpet snake — going along they been telling me about the yarn (Dreaming story) long time ago. Old people been going along, along, along — sleeping there — cooking big carpet snake and been went to sleep then and after that the sandhill all white. 'What this one here? Sandhill white?' Told me then — one man been cooking big carpet snake — big snake — mundu they call it — big carpet snake. 'They been killed this one here and they been run back and sleeping over there and burned that sandhill white.'

Every rockhole they been telling me names and all. You know, every rockhole got a name — they got blackfellas's names — another rockhole — another name. Another place called Italyu, another one called Mapa. That's blackfella's names. Rockholes everywhere. I been going along — I see the one, two, three holes and I was standing there, green, green, rainwater over there in the middle. Rainwater there in the middle on the side, another one that's green.

Every rockhole a story — old people — nice — when they tell stories.

They take a lot of sugar, tea leafs when they go out,

rock hole, rock hole and they digging big maku, digging around makus, they dig 'em out. Billy can full and sort of leafs like this one here (indicating bushy acacia tree) you see the sugar (lerps) and you hold the leaf — all white and you pull the leaf out and fill the big billy can and they go back and do like this, like that, like this, like that, put one leaf here, one leaf there and get the wool and tie 'em around then. Outside dry but nice and sweet inside — sweet. And when you go along you hear birds — oh — all sort of birds sing out when you go along — nice — in the trees — flying around — and you know where the sugar is and you come along and you see it all white on the leaves. This line here — Ooldea way — Immarna to Barton — you see nice ones again — like a banana — but the banana's a round one. This one here a little straight one — nice — you feel them — get the nice ones and cook 'em in the ashes. (Called *Mayaaka* in some places).

Sometimes you dig out roots — sometimes you see like a nice flat one — you cut them and sit down dig them then and when you cook them in the fire — hot ashes — you taste 'em like a potato. Audrey been eating them. We always cook 'em in the ashes. Another one they get real hot — little one like a onion — seen 'em — take all the little leaves off — all white inside.

And you see wild one — little small animal (marsupial mole) — small one. These all go under the sand — stand watching them — got to be quick — we digging them — they go through the little hole and come out there and we all standing in middle and go that-a-way, that-a-way — all the little kids — that way, that way — stand and watch 'em — he come out then another hole — ah we killed him — he must be dead — put 'em back again — all go under the sand. Little lizard — we always get that one there and go back. Put chewing tobacco (pitjuri — a mild narcotic) in mouth. Use 'em long time back and we all see that lizard going like this — like drunk — and we all laugh. Oh terrible long time we laugh — little lizards!

Tarcoola way, you know, Wynbring, Barton, Immarna, Ooldea — we always go back to Ooldea, always jump on the train, go to Watson and one girl again's

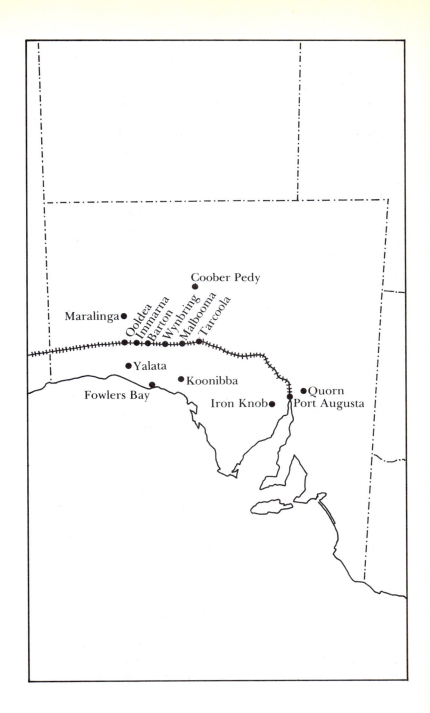

Coober Pedy

Maralinga

Ooldea
Immarna
Barton
Wynbring
Malbooma
Tarcoola

Yalata

Koonibba

Fowlers Bay

Iron Knob

Quorn
Port Augusta

been sick — Ooldea Home there — been die now — I been taking 'em — was very sick. I been jump on the train — we not pay nothing — jump on the tray — I been take 'em right to Cook Hospital — put 'em in there and I been come back then.

Mrs Dix was on the line then working. They was stopping at tank first when Beverley was little and after that shift into the railway house then — working on the railway. My uncle knew 'em. Mum's cousin too, he been come back and tell me 'Eh, good lady over there'. 'Where?' 'Ooldea — Christian woman — she give me water and all, and she have a little baby girl'. After that we been going over and have a look and playing with her kids — lot of kids went — got photos and all there.

Before, my old granny told me they always go out no blankets, no mattress, no billycan — only take water and put 'em on the head in container and thing underneath like I make (indicating a protective hair ring — like a cushion) — like that — big one — put them on head and go like that. Put the little babies on back — that's what they do — no blankets — but they make a nice (shelter), strong tree, you know cutting up when its raining — put a nice strong one — another one there, another one there, another one there, another one there and after that put the leaves — like that one there (acacia) — like tent when its up — and you know prickly one — take 'em from underneath — flatten them with the stick — rain won't come through, nothing. That's what they do long time ago and we have big fire — sleep anyway — no blankets.

No tea then, no sugar, nothing — they only go and shoot with the spear — come back with kuka — that's how they do — long time. They tell me everything — my granny — I been asking them lot of questions — old granny told to me you know. 'How you fellas do no billy can, no sugar?' 'No we have water, meat, no sugar, nothing, no coffees, just water, drink water that's all and meat'. Wild tuckers they get off the trees, that's all — long time ago — that's how they do it long time ago.

Ooldea — we come this way and dig sand — water — we digging — what happens — wait — water comes —

78

,pannikin been full. Lake Dey Dey, Fregon — same water again — same water there — dig 'em out — sit down and get rain water. Ooldea soakage still there — they got that right up. Got green water, trees, lawn, trees.

Audrey been born Immarna. Sandhills there. No doctor was there, nothing. I been born there — no doctors, Immarna — Barton in the sandhills. White fella was our father. He used to work on the railways. When I been get little bigger I always run to him when he come back from work — back to Barton there. He was in single man's cottages (at railway camp). They was up and down all the time. Father, white fella, been telling me when mum been single then, he was sitting down there and I was running — go to get a (bush) banana for my father.

I had a step-father too. My step-father even had another woman — west coast there and after that he went back Ooldea way. Mum there sitting down with me — won't forget that. And he reckon 'Oh I be your father — your mama.' Mama means father. 'I got to look after you, nguntu,' and I said 'No, what for?' and after that I was sitting down with my mum and said 'Mum, he too cheeky — got another woman — he got wife from west coast.' He left her, went back and got another one there.

After that, sitting down, sitting down, I was a big girl then, getting bigger and bigger. No kids then. I was sitting down before Gloria was born (Lorna's first daughter). Sitting down — going off getting the food, come back, up and down on the train — Ooldea, Tarcoola — come back. Gloria was born after Yalata and after that going around, going around, going around.

Tarcoola. One man get killed on the train. Another lot come, said 'Sit down, sit down.' 'Nyina, nyina' tell them like that you know. Can't talk English you know. Told them 'Nyina, nyina' No. Won't listen, train been going that way, turn around that way, bump into them. That man gone now, killed. After that another one again. Not very old then, was young. My old man was telling me. 'That man there, he won't listen. He gonna get killed that one on the train. Wanti.' He said 'Come over here — come back'. We sitting down then and another woman, cooking damper, big damper. That damper had crack in the middle. Anyone get killed on the train or someone get speared. There's hole when they cook damper. Split it in half in the ashes. Cut it all in bits and give it to dogs.

After that, sitting down, sitting down. One man, long whiskers — long whiskers and we know straight away then, long whiskers and lot of spears. He gonna get killed. Wynbring, another one again, everyone was crying. Old peoples crying, crying. That's true too. My old man been telling me. Get killed that way. They don't know the train. Don't look, sit down, don't listen.

I was promised to my old man (husband). When they put them over the rules, out in the bush they give my old man hiding and all that and they say 'malpa pikatja'. They been give me then. And after that I been sitting down then and another old man again Mabel's 'malpa pikatja'. They always give hiding — and when they give them hiding they give them 'malpa pikatja'.

There was one cheeky policeman then — Grosvenor. When we was Ooldea siding there, my old man been go out. He come back from the station. He got ten new blankets, everything — new clothes and he got cheque too. He come along and policeman chasing him then and he's running, running, running and he's got rifle too and he could see big tree — cut out tree — you know they cutting boomerangs and all — that sort of tree. He run and hide there then. Policeman been shooting him and after that he get cheeky and my old man got rifle, put the bullet in it — .33 bullet — blow the policeman's hat off. He been come back then and told me everything. After that he been station and the policeman turn around go back. Cheeky policeman too you know. He went to Tarcoola after that. We know that. Someone speared him. After that they been picking up two men, my old man and another one. They sent them to Adelaide. He go to Adelaide and tell them everything what Mr Grosvenor been doing. Tell them he burn all the new blankets, government blankets, billycans. Burn new blankets, everything. Shooting all the dogs. My old man been telling them there in Adelaide. Everything he been telling 'em. Him there two years and went back then.

They been shooting one man again this way. Policeman been shoot him. One dark one. We getting water and washing him. Raining, water on the ground there. Wash him, wash him. After that they was singing (to heal) that one there. Woman is singing and rubbing (massaging) then, make it better and they take him back.

After that I been looking around 'Where's Harold and Mabel — missing' and I looking around everywhere, everywhere, and everyone reckon 'No, they been taken back that-a-way. From Malpuma they went back to Wynbring.' I been jump on the train then. Jump on the truck. When the cars come then I been hide. The whistle go then. Save the two kids again (Mabel and Harold), jump down Wynbring again, jump down and see the two kids was standing there. Mabel and Harold — nuisances. Mum took Mabel to Coorabie there then, in the camp.

When I been bigger I went with my promised husband. I was big girl then. He been growing me up. Twelve, thirteen when I went with my husband. My husband had other wives but he leave 'em. And from there we been sitting down. My old man they all call 'malpa pikatja' but my mother had nothing to do with it see, my old man, he call me out.

Before that, long time ago, I'll tell you my time, about Gloria's father. I been go with that one there first. (This must have been after Lorna was promised but before she actually lived with her 'old man'). He want to try and marry me. I'll tell you. That's long time. He want to try and marry me. He bush fella too but he won't drink. I left him. I wasn't getting married to him. He reckons 'I take you to Adelaide, get married.' I run away then. You know what I was thinking? I was thinking of mum. I can't leave 'em. See I take mum around everywhere.

I got Richard, Jeffrey and Thelma by my old man, promised one. Gloria's father went to Adelaide. I wasn't getting married to him. He good fella though. He won't drink, won't drink. I was thinking about mum. Got to

81

stay with mum. Sad you know. Feel sorry for mum, you know.

Out in the bush I tell you — no hospital there — they have baby in the camp. All my kids born in the camp and anybody when they have a baby in the camp — doctor nothing — just womans. They sit down around. They putting the baby's head down. Doing it like that. Putting the baby down and the baby get born. That's true. In the hospital they put you down (lay down — not squat) but this one here the women make 'em sit up — easier. They put arm around and straighten the baby. Might be head up here and they put the head down, feel 'em, feel it, feel 'em and the head down then. Get ready. Woman straighten 'em.

They got long cord and they cut small and after that when they're babies and they put hot ashes, not proper really hot, feel it and they put it there. Put their tummy right see and they put hot ashes and put it like this then — push 'em like that (umbilical cord) and after that they cut it — dry — finished. It's way they do and they get that little string on there. The baby won't cry then.

I can do everything — spinning. I was watching them long time ago, when I had no kids. I thought 'What they putting there?' And they tell me. Soak it in the water and put 'em around like that for little girls — boys have different one. They make with rabbit fur, feather, rabbit hair, spinning it, and they put it around here for the boys (around waist, not neck like girls) and the boys won't cry — sleep all day. Clever isn't it? And they lay down and when they cry — sleep like that — in the sand in the bush and when the baby's sleeping they put sand on its tummy. Baby won't get up and cry for you. Lay down anyway. Won't cry. Three or four days — won't cry. Only for milk, that's all, that time they won't use bottles. All my kids (breastfed).

We carry them (in a sling), I'll show you. I'll make one. I want to give to Audrey. Cut little piece of rag and I make 'em and put a bit of string on and make nice little soft thing and put the baby down there and you can put 'em on back or on here (front) and tie the little seat on it. Long time ago when they having baby out that-a-way —

no houses — they carry baby like that (in a large wooden dish) like they carry water. That's a long time ago — no blankets. When they get a little bit bigger, they put 'em on the back then so that how they go for walk. Mine I always tie 'em with the blankets to me.

We always walk around. Go on the camels, just on the camels. When Gloria was little — jump on the camels. When the camels get up say 'Give me that tjitji' — kid you know. 'Want tjitji'. When the camel start up they give me Gloria on the lap and get started then — go along. Gloria sitting up — big camel saddles — water and everything on them. I can ride on the camels. We always travel, travel, travel, travel to other places. We leave the camels, have a spell, help the camels up, let go the camels, you know, the bell ringing. Go and get them. About six or seven camels we had. Lot of camels. Take a lot of blankets and all, everything, water. There was my old man, my uncle and auntie, big mob, lot of them. Some walk. When feel tired you can jump on the camel.

We go around to (pastoral) stations. Work on the stations. Everyone travel around. Old man was working — fencing. We travel around with the old people. Old people all finished. We go around to another station, another station, they give the ration out. No money was that time there. No pension was that time then. No social service or nothing. They give ration out when we ask 'em. They give 'em. That's how they do.

Ration day we always go clean. Big lump of sugar. Standing there, big lump of sugar. 'That's for lollies' they say. We always put 'em in the bag. Sugar for tea. We been on Tarcoola when they been giving rations out.

We been stopping there and they reckon they can see that big cave there. Big cave with the women singing that song (Dreaming story). That one there that's two sisters. That's a story about two sisters going back from here. Remember that hill. You know the women dancing, singing. Those women, going along, going along, stop there, another one sister was standing and the youngest one was crying then, crying, crying, crying. Cave there, side of Tarcoola. Other side, man's cave.

I remember about Maralinga. Out there with the bomb. They been tell them 'Oh, they gonna send rocket, you fellas be careful now, look at the wind.' Another lot thinking, another lot thinking, another lot thinking. 'Oh, the wind turned, the wind gone up that-a-way — its lucky, we get safe.' We was over there. Wind blew it to Indulkana way then. We was up this way, west coast. Everybody been come this way see. From Ooldea, Ooldea closer to Maralinga and they been shift from Maralinga to Yalata and we was at mission, Koonibba. We come through before and after that another lot come this way. Another lot gone west. They drive them all back west. MacDougall was there. We know MacDougall. There was two, that other one had broken arm. MacDougall wanted to help 'em.

Mum been bring Audrey down mission there. Stay in mission there. Policeman drive all back from there. That's when they shift them. Smoke. Sent that smoke. That's when Lallie and them get 'em, from Indulkana. I been come this way, Bookabie way, stay on the station. We been stopping out Ooldea way on the line and from there Fowlers Bay.

My mum put Audrey in the home, — learn school and all that. From there the mission home, sitting down when I been come down with Gloria. After that they send her to Adelaide then, college. Nurse then. That's how was learnt. When Audrey come back, working in the hospital here then. Working in the man's ward.

Long time ago, no rifles, they use spear for rabbits, my old man used spear too. My old man been going along and two dogs. Leave 'em home. I tell him no good taking dogs in the hot and he get a spear then. Two spears and go along. They can spear kangaroo. If kangaroo's sleeping they come along then with the spear. Good shots. That's what they do long time ago. Spear better than rifle. When babies were little.

They're all grown up now. Gloria got four girls and one boy. My other daughter Thelma, got only two. Another son Jeffrey, he got one, a girl, just went back Adelaide. My old man, I was born a Cobby first before and my old man, he come down, west coast way. One man, one white man get 'im. 'My name is Tom Grant-hams. You'll be Bobby Grantham'. One white fella 'You're my brother.' Reckons he's brother to my old man. 'You'll be Grantham. You're Bobby. Bobby — Robert Grantham.' It how he got his name. My old man. Nankara, his Aboriginal name. When Miss Lock was there. He's the one been giving name me. My mum was May Cobby. We got whitefella father, me and Audrey. See, mine, my father was there working Barton, on the line and finished and go away Adelaide or somewhere. Died I suppose somewhere. I go run over there all the time when I was little, sitting down all the time at the table. My mother was sitting out in the scrub. We're living in the scrub. I know my father.

But after that, we never would have been living with him. Our step-father, he been living with mum then. He from west coast. All the same. He grow 'em up like a father, me. I like him too, good. My step-father 'I'll grow you up'. Mum living with my stepfather. Tell 'em straight then. 'I'll live with your mother.' Audrey taken away when she was little, Mabel knows.

I been come down when mum was here mission, Koonibba Mission. Mum was there, I come down with one kid, was Gloria. Stop with mum then. Audrey was in the mission there and I say 'Where's Audrey?' Mum reckon, 'Put 'em in the home' 'Where?' 'Mission, Koonibba, went in home.'

Working on the fences after. Working Bookabie way right around, working, fencing. Get paid too you know. No rations. Fowlers Bay, policeman giving ration out, Fowlers Bay, blankets, everything they was giving out. Fowlers Bay, good place, good fishing too, nice. Left my mother when I was a big girl, living with my old man then.

Mum used to visit Audrey in the home. Always see Audrey in the home there. From there they reckon going to send Audrey away. Mum was there crying for Audrey. Don't know what Audrey was going to do. You know mum was crying. When we walk around, walk around, rabbiting, walk around, 'What you crying for?' Worrying for Audrey too. Crying all the time, all the time. 'I can't see her now they send her to Adelaide.' That's what mum's thinking, you know, that's true too. Long time after, Audrey in this hospital here then, in man's ward. I was in the hospital too. I been stopping in the reserve there and after that (nursing) sister been coming around to see me. 'Hey, you Audrey's sister.' She seen my face, you know. 'Hey, you Audrey's sister.' Me oldest. 'I can see Audrey and you same.' Long time ago. I was in the hospital then. Poor mum.

We can't find mum. We crying, crying for mum all the time. Mum went missing. Terrible, ini? When you lose the mother, you know. I had to look after my old man. Have to look after him properly but he drink. My old man, too much drinking all the time. Getting old too.

I been come to Port Augusta when Jeffrey was in Adelaide. I left, Jeffrey was born here. I come out and take Jeffrey down to Adelaide, my baby son. Leave him there and come back. We been stopping there and went back because we got no house. We was stopping in the sandhills there first at the reserve there. From there then went down and when we come back, white man give 'em a house then, give 'em a house and put in for pension for me and my old man. After that we been getting pension then and after that, white man gone then.

Jeffrey was in Adelaide. I left him there. He been grow up there then. His feet was bent in, you know, bent to side. That's how we left him there. He be born like that. He was in the hospital. They look after him. You know nurses, sisters, and all. That's where he grow up. He be going back there soon. He's got a girlfriend now. Got a little baby. He's here now. He been come back for Christmas, after Christmas staying with me and went back again. He don't like it stopping here. He like Adelaide more better. City boy I suppose.

We left the camels, someone sell 'em. Left them when we come this way. My uncle had a lot of camels. We travelled mostly around Ooldea way. Right around, Ooldea, right up Coober Pedy. Right around to Ingomar, right over to Tringana, that's the way we travel around. White fellas give 'em jobs. We sit down there, do work and after we finished, we go other place, work for a little while, get 'em rations. Work, they do fencing, shearings and all that. They learn fencing, netting, dog fence, my old man. We go everywhere.

I been Adelaide but the white people look after me. I might get lost. I take Jeffrey down there when he's a little baby. Left 'em and then I come back, went back that-a-way, west coast way, come back again. I always make 'em thing, put 'em on head, wool, you seen them in the pictures. I was doing them. I can spin that one there too, rabbit fur, but they been giving me that sheep wool and spinning 'em, but I like rabbit fur.

One woman on the roadhouse, I was standing there, they were travelling, white women, travelling and they go past and they buy these things. They ask me, 'What they do with this?' I been get a spear and a woomera and hook 'em on the spear and I been showing them how they kill rabbits and all that. I been telling them, waddy, tuck 'em under here, tie them to the belt. But they don't know. I been telling them everything.

They gave me big packet of lollies, but I never eat the lollies. I go back and give the kids the lollies. Next time when I go back to Yalata, I'll get a spear, woomera, come back and show 'em then. You mustn't let the woomera go, you let the spear go, I been telling them, you do it like this. You can't hold this spear and hold this woomera. Hold this woomera and let this spear go. After that, 'What they do with this one here?' Boomerang. Take this boomerang too, do circle that boomerang, come back, come back. My old man always chucked the boomerangs. Go round, round and round, and come back again. When the boomerang come, catch it quick. When the boomerang come back too quick, move like that.

I like telling people about the way we used to live.

Lallie Lennon

Lallie was born in the northwest of SA and has had a very difficult life. Her European father died when his underground house collapsed after heavy rain. Lallie worked as a child on a station and was treated quite cruelly. Later, when she had young children, she and her family were very ill after being exposed to the fallout from the nuclear bomb tests in the Maralinga lands. They still suffer today and have never received any compensation. Lallie now works as an Aboriginal health worker in Port Augusta and is a grandmother.

Maralinga Dust

I was married at the time with three children, and my husband, Stan was doing fencing at Mabel Creek Station. We came down and it was a new Ghan running then — first time — used to be old steam engine — I came down on the steam engine. We was that pleased to get in this flash new Ghan — hiding our billy cans and all that — anyway kids were crying and we were trying to stop people looking — we was embarrassed I think — I was anyway — the billy can dropped out and we'd try to hide it. Banjo Walkington and his wife were on the train with us. She was carrying too I think.

We were going back to Mabel Creek. We got off at Kingoonya and got a ride with Mr Dingle, mail driver, he had all this petrol — right up high it was — forty-four gallon drums — some underneath and some on top — and I was big — just about to go in. Anyway had to climb all the way up there — got off the train and had to get on these drums — I don't think they cared about Aboriginal woman sitting on drums — he was only a boy, Mr Dingle — and I had to hold on to the kids — Stan wouldn't do it — they all sitting in the front there — and I'm holding on there — 'can't you hold this?' — asking Stan. 'Oh shut up!' he answers. Anyway — I just had to put up with it and kids' behinds was burnt with petrol — the petrol was leaking — mine was burnt with petrol — one place and I can't move with big stomach and trying to hold on to the kids and ropes — you know ropes was tied to hold on to the drums — it was very cruel. Anyway we got to no 7 and they said 'come in for a cup of tea Dingle.' Anyway — they went in — and one woman came out but I couldn't get down I was stiff and everything — burnt — skin was burnt — petrol — and I was so wild with Stan — anyway they got down and got their scones and that and cup of tea — I had my cup of tea up top there with the kids.

Anyway we got started back to Mabel Creek — got off

89

A truck like that which Lallie and her children had to sit on the back of when she was pregnant.
Photo by Len Beadell.

Lallie Lennon with son Bruce. Stan Lennon on right.

12 o'clock in the night I suppose — gee I was pleased to get off — so burnt with this petrol. Put vaseline on ourselves and all — so wild with Stan — anyway we stayed there for a while. We lived down the Creek — I was ready to go in — I said 'can't I go back to Port Augusta?' — baby's ready.' I shouldn't have went to Mabel Creek. Anyway lived in the creek there — I thought oh well if I have the baby — if anything happens it doesn't matter — no help see — anyway baby starts giving me pain — that was '53 — anyway I went up the creek and had the baby myself — cut the cord and that — kept it wrapped up like that. Stan never gave a cup of water or anything — I just had to stay there. I thought Aboriginal women have them like this — I might as well be like them — stayed there for a while and Mavis brought some water and that. I had Jasol with me but I didn't have water see.

That was when trucks was going through with these big things — didn't know what that was. I was ready to go home then with the baby — and all these big trucks going through — and all these people you know — dressed up — uniforms. They were everywhere. I didn't know what was going on and they had a big thing on top of a rise there and I was in camp then — dust was getting on us from the trucks going through. Stan goes up to the station but never comes back and tell me what it was — when I try to ask he says 'Oh I dunno, just trucks that's all.' I just live along like that — anyway next minute this big war tank went past — first time we saw it — guns sticking out you know — was frightening — I thought — I wonder if they're going to kill us. I kept thinking to myself — because I couldn't get anything anywhere. 'Oh they're going that way doing tests on bombs.' Mavis said — what Stan told her. Anyway stayed down the creek for a little while. Stan was walking around with them — that was a long way from us — anyway they went on.

They said they're bombs. After that when they went up — a few days after — they said, 'Bombs going to go off directly.' Mavis said Stan told her they going to let a test go and I said, 'Oh gee it's going to blow us up.' I was scared — I said, 'Well what's going to happen?' 'Oh it's just going to go off — we'd better watch it you know.' I was frightened — getting up there and worrying about the kids — what's going to happen — they'd be screaming — thinking you know. I supposed they'd be screaming and thinking and running to me — I don't know. That was just going through my mind. Everybody else wasn't worried but I didn't know much see. Tried to ask Stan and it was nothing — so I just live along like that. I thought well if it goes off it goes off.

Anyway we were watching out for this in the afternoon — must have been about 3 or 4 — we all watching you know and I was thinking I wonder if it's going to blow us up. It went off and a big rumble came on through — all right around — big noise — rumble — ground's shaking and everything. Anyway — saw this big mushroom thing go off and it just laid there, you know, in the sky — it was just like a white sky — like a cloud — you see a wide cloud just laying there — was just like that — next day when we got up that was gone.

Anyway, after that, I'm not sure if it was three weeks or two weeks we went back to Mintabie. Anyway this bomb — they was talking about they was going to let another one off — I wasn't worried then because I knew it was going to go up like the other one. Anyway we went back to Mintabie for a holiday looking around for opals. June was only little. She might have been just starting to walk — I don't know so far back. Went back there and was looking around for opals.

We had our breakfast — got up early because we was anxious to look for opals. Had our breakfast. 'Bombs going up again this morning.' Oh yeah. I was thinking long way from the bomb now. You know I wasn't so frightened. 'Oh yes it's going to go off this morning.' We listen to the little wireless we carried around. We had our breakfast and washed up our things — put 'em all away and it's nearly time to go off now — we was watching out for it — made that same kind of noise only it was bit closer this time. It sounded a bit close but we couldn't see it — we was in a hollow — could only see the top of it. Little while after — didn't take long — suppose it'd be about 7 — you can see the smoke coming through the trees and the sky going — you know blowing — blowing through. It was sort of slow down the bottom coming but up the top it was sort of going fast. But oh gee, anyway we could smell the gunpowder and Alec Woody was there with us and none of us were too sure. He said quick put the rag over your nose and he had a hanky over his nose — he was scared of it — was laughing.

Anyway at the same time I was looking around for this tree — it had sugar in it you know and I was going to suck it — like honey always runs down — I was going to give it to the kids and Alec said, 'Don't touch that — it could be poison.' Lucky he did. That's when I noticed the dust was on the trees. Sort of a grey-black, you know — not much — but you can see it on the trees — how it settled. That could be poison he reckoned — don't touch em. Anyway I wouldn't touch it — got frightened of it. It was only through him — I was a bit scared — it was making me scared — that could be poison you know — white fellas letting these things off. I never thought like that. And Stan said Ah! — he was laughing — he went up on top of the hill trying to look for some opals. But oh gee, anyway — it was that time the kids starting getting sick — you know vomiting and rash and I thought they're getting flu — forgot about the bomb — they must be getting flu again and I sort of felt sickish you know and then kids were vomiting — all that. They had little bit of rash — sort of a red — and I'd bath them in the water — we wasn't allowed to use too much water — only one drum of water we had — and if the truck breaks down we mightn't get water for weeks, so I just washed them in a dish and put their same dirty clothes back on — it wasn't worth it — red dirt. Anyway — I said, 'These kids are getting sick,' and June was only little and she was sort of taking a fit or something — jumping — I think she was overheated or something — too hot — anyway we packed our things and came back to Mabel Creek — Welbourn Hill. We came back and I was telling Joan how these kids was sick. Anyway she said why don't you give them something — I gave

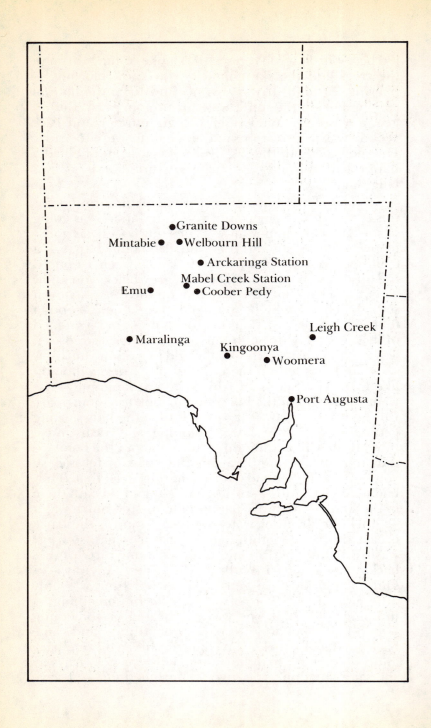

them castor oil before I came away because I only had a little bit in the bottle — thought this'll clean their stomach out anyway — I thought — gave them that and told Mrs Giles that they was sick and that and told her must be flu, bit of a dry cough you know — I didn't feel too good neither.

Anyway she said, keep on taking the castor oil. She gave me another bottle and she gave us — it's a brown stuff — you put two drops in the sugar — I know the name of it — I can't say it. It's for cold or anything like that. Or if you have a big cut you put that on — that brown stuff. It's not iodine — it's that other one like iodine — pretty smell I reckon it's pretty smell. Friar's Balsam! Yeah — that's what we were having all the time. Anyway we were travelling on to Mabel Creek — I had dysentery — kids had dysentery — all sick — it was terrible. Anyway we got there late so we camped in the creek and I was so sick with this, you know. I told Stan to get something from the station and they gave me these white tablets to stop the dysentery — gave us some of that — take it four times a day or something you know — couldn't understand anyhow — take them anyhow. It helped. Jennifer wasn't too good at all — she was so sick. She just sort of didn't know us — she was looking at herself — looking at her hand — looking at everyone's hand — she was sort of funny. I was worried. And June was taking fits. I had handful.

We wanted to go in Coober Pedy. Stan started growling, 'I don't know what you're running around for.' I said, 'There's no doctors there's no nothin'.' I wanted help because station people — they don't help that much — didn't even come down and see us. That Mary Rankin she never come down and see what was wrong with us. Anyway I wasn't satisfied — I wanted to go in Coober Pedy. Stan took me in there — wasn't happy — but I was worried about the kids. We went in there and Mrs Brewster gave us cough mixture and said if they still take them turns bath them in mustard water — so I was doing that — mustard water — tablespoon full in this water. See I didn't know them people you see. Only she was a shopkeeper — Mrs Brewster. I don't know

95

what she was she just told me to put them in the mustard bath and that's what I done and they were really sick.

I didn't know what to do — I thought oh well — just carry on look after them like that and then she gave us eucalyptus. 'If that brown stuff not making them any better give them eucalyptus in sugar — together — mix it up together and rub them all over with olive oil and eucalyptus — or don't give them eucalyptus — give them olive oil — plenty olive oil with this sugar.' They just eat it — you know — they loved it. They couldn't eat much — just giving them milk — bring it up, you know. Jennifer was taking fits. June was taking fits. It was so hard for me. It must have been only a few days — no, a week after those tests.

We came right through in a Blitz. That's a big truck — an army truck — Stan had that — that was Stan's father's. Truck — *old Blitz* they called it and we had a little house on it — sort of like a tent on it and we had the tank under the campsheet too, tied around the drum — just get on the drum and up into the tent. We was living in that. Must have been a week they was sick. Think we only had one night from Mintabie. Welbourne Hill — then we had — I can't remember — I think we camped from Mintabie somewhere along the road there — next day we got to Welbourne Hill and from there we got to Mabel Creek and then Coober Pedy — and they were sick then all the time.

They were sort of weakish — I was sick myself — old woman was looking after two kids — old Toddy — she used to live in the dugout — so she helped me out with the kids. She took one. She's old lady, she was, and I didn't know her — a stranger but she helped me. She said, 'I'll look after the baby while you look after the other ones.' That was good help — and she used to rub them up and put them to bed. I was worried because she was in the dugout you know — inside — thought they might suffocate but they were okay. I used to go in and have a look — they used to go down the stairs and then go in like that. She helped me out. Barney was there with his mob but they were okay — it was only us who were sick.

96

I remember this bloke MacDougall he was trying to take the people away from Maralinga — shift them away — because he knew the tests — he didn't like it — he didn't like it at all — but they just done it. He was working hard: never used to preach or nothing. He went up there and he tried to tell them people and he couldn't understand their language and that kind of thing but he had a — he reckoned he had an old man there — he was talking for him — Maralinga — all around there — he was so tired trying to tell them people to keep away — big fire was coming he was trying to tell them — and they reckon the people — soon as he came away went back that way somewhere. Telling the people to get going and them people went back and they never seen them people again — that's what I heard. Mr MacDougall was talking about it and Mr Bartlett was there. He was so tired poor thing — on his own. Had red — no had blond hair. Had fair skin and freckles — poor thing. He tried his best. He came back when everything was finished — he got all these people and took them to Woomera — we had to go and get our chests done and that. I think it was for TB that test. X-ray kind of thing. They never told us what it was for. I got this rash thing but they wouldn't tell me about it. I've still got that rash — go on until I die. On our heads too. I went down talking to them about it and they don't want to tell me. Tell me my father had it and my father *didn't* have it. We can't use soap — skin comes off. Bruce is bad, worse than I am. Bruce was outside with me — we both got the rash. Jennifer was playing with the baby inside the tent when that was happening — I had Bruce on my arm — watching.

There were other people around but we didn't mix with them. That Giles from Welbourn Hill, he died from cancer on his liver. Mrs Giles'd have a story to tell. The smoke went over them too. She was worrying about her orange trees. Orange trees don't look too good — Wonder if that smoke's doing that. After that again we went back.

We're always going back that way because we were lonely. We didn't know it was dangerous — just thought it was bombs going off. Mr MacDougall used to help get injections for the kids — and Mr Bartlett — they were so good to the Aboriginal people — they were the only ones.

Miriam Dadleh

Miriam's mother, an Aranda woman, was born at Hermannsberg in the NT and her father came from Peshawar in Pakistan as a camel driver. Miriam spent her early years travelling through Australia with her father's camel team, getting to know Aboriginal people and their cultures as she travelled. She settled at various times in Alice Springs, Oodnadatta, Marree and Port Augusta where she now lives. Miriam has recently suffered from a stroke and was in hospital when I last heard news of her. Miriam is a great grandmother.

Fair Devil Sticky Beak

I was born at a place called Henbury Station in the Northern Territory, about 74 year ago on the eleventh of September, 1910. I'm Aranda — half and half — Aranda and Afghan. Dad was a camel driver see and he used to pull up at Alice Springs for a fortnight or three weeks while I go to school there so I won't forget my schooling. We lived in Oodnadatta — we had a home in Oodnadatta. I went up to Grade 6.

I had eight kids. Wait there, I might be wrong — er seven — one girl and six boys. I had three boys living for a long time — I lost three — that's six boys and one girl. One girl was Mrs Fielding, and one son is Ken Dadleh and there's Dean Mahomed, managing the Aboriginal hostel here, see I was married twice. With my first husband (Gool Mahomed) I got Mrs Fielding and Dean Mahomed and two boys I lost. I lost them as baby you know — 7 months, 8 months. The other two are Dadleh, husband called Noor 'Lulla' Dadleh. When I was younger, I used to be sticky beak — asking people. I used to go around asking people. See, if I saw a lot old women up there, I'll go and see what they gathered for, what they there for and they used to tell me. They even told when the women was having babies, asked me to come over and see. 'Come on girl you might come and see this one.' I used to go and sit down and watch what they gonna do. When the little baby's born they get a root of a tree and skin that — get that and tie the little cord, they take it up tight and get a stone knife and cut it and the other women would pluck their hair and start weaving it, make like a string. See one time they used to have a band around, when they cut the cord — bandage around — some used to put a button or cut a cardboard about 20c size — so belly button won't come out — used to put a bandage around. They make a cloth for dingle-dangle — cover it. They put string then, just like knitting wool, that's human hair or rabbit's fur — they weave it. They clean the baby in the sand, if they do the number one. When they do number two they wipe it with sand — warm sand when the baby's born — they make a hot fire, take all the coals away and just mix it up with sand in it — that's how they used to dry the kid — the kid never get blisters or sore like today — see I think too many chemical and stuff make them sore — Aboriginal never had any medicine — bush medicine. I used to go and find out. I used to go when I see old Aboriginal women sitting around — stickybeaking and ask.

Dad didn't want us to mix up, but he was real glad one day — we nearly got perished. We went round in circles I don't know how many times — come back to the same spot — go again — come back in the same spot — go away for a couple of hours — back in the same spot. We met an old Aboriginal man — he had a belt on with rabbits and mulku. I thought this is no good, me and my brother, that brother there (indicating photo) me and him, I told him, I said, 'I'm going to ask this old man. I'll speak lingo and ask this old tjilpi to show us the way to Tyone Station.' This is in South Australia — inside the border. I'm asking him and he told me he had rabbit — kuka rabita, kuka mulku (rabbit meat, cat meat). He wanted to give me one and I said 'No' I was frightened you know. Cat! (laughs). And then I ask him, I said, 'Could you tell us the way to Tyone Station? We went and came back here same place,' He said, 'You know mamu country? You never chuck'm stone. That's what make you come back — lot o' dead people around here.'

It must be true because we went out and come back three or four times and he said, 'Come here, come here piccaninny.'

My Dad said, 'What's he goin' to show us there?' I said, 'Never mind Dad he's asking us to come. He's goin' to show us something.'

He took us over the sandhills and showed us this mark. You can still see that mark — you know — old wagon wheel, where it went through in the wet weather and how it left like a ridge. He said 'You take this one (in his language — that's a ridge that's everlasting. You follow this — it'll take you straight to Tyone.' He said

'When you come to another sandhill — you can't see it — the sand buried that ridge — go on over other side — look around you see it again.' When we came to the sandhill Dad said, 'The bugger — he telling lies — tracks finish here.' I said, 'Well he told us. We go to other side now, look around.' So my little brother go over and look around.

Anyhow we went over to find out, 'Here's that track again.' Took us right to the place he told us — Tyone Station. We got lost because we didn't throw stone at well — water there. He reckon if we'd thrown stones there we wouldn't of got lost. Kumpiti, like a ghost or something, some sort of spirit. You gotta throw stone and it won't harm you. They reckon big snake, kumpiti inside in that water.

Aroona Dam too, near Copley, they had one there. A stranger go, you see, the water come out — rush out — you throw stone — the water calm. But they must have killed the snake see. They cemented that spring, Aroona Dam, to keep a storage of water. Old people reckon they must of killed that snake. That must've been true because it happened to us — keep on coming back and coming back. Old Tjilpi put us on right track and he was saying something in his lingo — praying or something — puts us on the track and that track took us up to Tyone Station.

I was a fair devil then. I was a fair devil when I was young — we wasn't allowed to go to the corroboree, you know, not half-castes see. They used to tell us 'No half-castes allowed to go this corroboree.' There was a half-caste boy, Henry Dixon, and me and I used to say 'What about you and me go, see what's going on?' Me and him followed these people and they'd pull up and say, 'Go on — get back. Not allowed to follow us.' And we'd sit down and we'd see they gone a bit further away and get up and run again. They might go about three or four hundred yards and stop and look back — 'Can't see them two.' We'd duck down. When we got to the corroboree — they was all sitting around in circle and the men was painted up. Me and him sneaked up and we went up to these old women. They were so afraid, poor old things. 'You going to get us killed — you shouldn't come.' 'Too late we're here now.' Poor old things covered us up with blanket. I seen everything what was going on by lifting the blanket. Soon as the old men go back and get dressed, me and him used to take off — back to the town. When the women catch up to us they'd say 'You know if they'd a seen you two — we would'a got killed.' I said 'Yes, and I can tell you everything that was going on.' (laughs). True, I used to be fair devil.

It was very strict, girls or women not allowed to see anything, man's corroboree or anything. Only when they have their dances, that's when you see them, but you not allowed to ask them, just like Buffalo Lodge see. There's no women allowed to go to Buffalo Lodge, only men. They got their own secrets, where women don't know. They can't even tell their own wives what's goin' on in Buffalo Lodge. My two brothers was in the Lodge and their wives used to ask them what they did. 'We're not allowed to tell youse.' Aboriginal people too, their tribal laws just like Lodge people. Women not allowed to know anything, girls not allowed to know. I used to be sticky beak and ask.

I was born in 1910 and my brother Rocky was born in 1913 and the other one in 1918. Our mother passed away in 1919. My mother travelled around with my father with that camel train from Oodnadatta right up to Wauchope, Burnham, Hatches Creek. We used to go with my father. He was a hawker. Had his own business. When he get rid of his groceries, return journey he used to pick up mica about 18 inches long, about 6 inch wide. Wolfram — take two person to lift it — that heavy — metal, iron or something. Wolfram, I had a piece but someone borrowed it — take 'em to school or take 'em somewhere — but not here — it was in Marree that wolfram I had. I had quartz here but it got legs and went away somewhere.

My mother was brought up in a mission, see.

From a little girl she was brought up in the mission and then after schooling, she was reading, writing in English, German, Aranda and Dieri too. At Hermannsberg — I suppose you heard of Mr Strehlow — Profes-

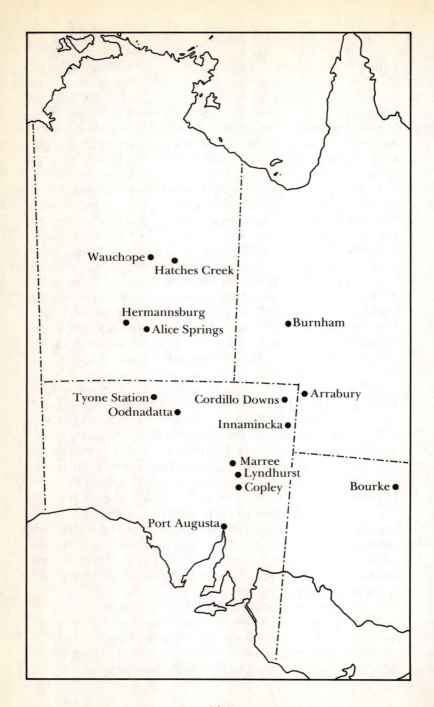

sor Strehlow — his father — he reared my mother. He died at Horseshoe Bend, in 1922, I can remember that, just after my mother died.

I was never brought up in the mission home or with the Aboriginals. I was with my father. Father never left us with anybody. When mum passed away he reared us himself. Brother of mine was only a baby, 12 months, 18 months old. He was brought up on the camel's milk — that's why he's so tall I think. He used to stand up underneath the camels and suck. We used to stand around by him and you see that cow camel — they hold their milk back, but in a little while they'd be bursting. He used to stand there sucking away and me and my other brother used to try and bludge on him. Soon as he got full we'd get a pannikan or fruit tin and we used to hold it and get it full for us.

Afghan people never let their kids go. The police used to come to take us away and my father said 'No. They're my kids and I'm going to rear them.' They said 'You're a man, you're travelling.' He said 'I can look after them. I can take time off to cook their tucker.' He used to sew our clothes and all — poor old thing.

He was 82 or could've been more when he died. 1950 my father passed away, in August and Jamesie was born in September. That's 34 years ago.

My father came out to Australia in 1892, 2nd November, on a ship called *Landsdowne Tower*. It was a French boat, landed here in Port Augusta. Then he travelled overland to Bourke, New South Wales. He came with the camels — he had countrymen from the same country — none of his brothers. He lost his brother — they had a bit of a charity and a feast at home and he got choked eating rice. When he died, dad come away. He ran away from home then he went to India and come out here.

Aboriginal people and one of his own countryman's son was working too for him. Afghan boy, real Afghan too, not like us part ones, his cousin's son. The Aboriginal people were from the north. Two my mother's brothers was working for him and my cousin, my mother's sister's son and young English-European lad working for us. Some from Oodnadatta, along the track. He had two strings of camels. He had a cousin's son drive one team and he got the other one. They used to call them strings of camels.

A camel train near Oodnadatta.
Photo from Bagot and Marsh Collection.
Archival Negatives Aboriginal Heritage Unit.

My name was Khan — not billy can — watercan (laughs). My father told us lot about his country, told his way of speaking his language — forget a lot. Now when people come here and speak to me I can speak back a bit — no-one here to talk Afghan to. There's only two or three can talk Afghan. My brother, Akbar and my brother Rocky and me. All these other part Afghans — they can't speak — three or four of them. My father's brother was a priest and his sons can't talk, yet they can pray Afghan prayer. A lot don't want to say they're Afghan — come from Afghan father and black mother. Just because their skin is lighter they're 'white' people — but whitefellas know you've got black blood in you.

I'm proud of my black people. I go back to Hermannsberg and talk to people — stay there couple of weeks or two or three months. I can talk Aranda. I can talk Luritja, understand Pitjantjatjara, bit of Dieri, bit of Arabana. I can talk my father's language. I like learning languages.

When I was at school I used to wag it a bit — used to go in the sheepyards. Sheepyard not far from Police Station. Me and Rocky used to get in sheepyards and dad got a notice from school that me and him never come, asking 'What's wrong? She never come to school two or three days.' Dad said 'Well every morning she

106

leaves here for school and her brother.' So the Policeman's watching us one day — seen us going in the sheepyards — never see us come out of that yard. He come down there with a whip. Poor old Rocky went cruising out of the way and I run straight back to school and he run home.

You see whenever we go past these sheepyards you see a lot of lambs there so we used to be like all kids — we went in to play with the lambs — we forgot about school — played with the lambs. Now and again I'd pinch him or hit him and he'd start to cry over the lamb. We'd be fighting over the lamb.

When my father fell in love with my mother at Hermannsberg they ran away. My grandfather said 'You can have my daughter' and they ran away. They made a mistake when they got on the border though — the Territory and South Australia — Police was waiting for them. He had to take my mother back all the way back to Hermannsberg. He didn't want to leave her. Thought living together a child might come along — something like that. He had to go to Alice Springs to get married in the Registry Office. Mr Stott was the Sergeant there. Mr Stott was still there when I was a woman. I don't know how many years he was there — for a long time — very old man. I went to school with his children.

Them days see no Northern Territory Aboriginal woman's allowed to come down to South Australia. Had to have a permit or some little thing like that and if any white man married a black woman, they had to marry them, they couldn't just live with them, they had to marry them before they could take them across the border. Well my father had to marry my mother before he could bring her over the South Australian border from the Northern Territory border. He did come close up to the border but he was still on the Northern Territory side when they caught them.

Lot of memories of old days in Oodnadatta sneaking away to the corroboree. Us kids used to go down to the dam and we used to paint and corroboree ourselves then — get in trouble too. Chinese market garden there

107

on that side of Oodnadatta. We used to live the other side — Nor-West of the town. The South side they had a big garden. Ah-chee family. That Chinaman had three children. His wife was half-caste old woman too. Ah-Chee people here in Port Augusta now. He was a real old Chinaman.

I was 18 when I got married to my first husband. He was Gool Mohamed. We was sneaking around — same as these lot do now (laughter). Well — tell the truth, if our mother — father know — step-mother know — might give me bullet or cut my throat or something — sneak around. It got that strong me and him run away next. We ran away from Lyndhurst Siding there. Afghan people have to catch you before you — you know. But my father said we can't reach them now — let them go. We sneaked out — we went straight to the Presbyterian Minister. Muntji: I told them there — told them I was 21 and we got married that night. I said we had to get married because we not allowed to sleep together unless we got married — that poor old minister — he bustled around there and married us there at Beltana.

Well we must have travelled about 70 odd miles. My husband was just like me — mother come from same country and father come from Peshawar and my mother was full-blood — his mother was part. We lived in Beltana and I had my first child there. I went back to Oodnadatta and I had a boy that I lost, then another boy again that I lost, then Dean. I had good luck with that son and after he's 2 year old I got married again and we had two more sons then, Ken and the other one I lost.

I met my second husband, 'Lulla', at Marree there. I regret it — because we was drunk. Well I own up. I never beat behind bushes and take this and that — I say everything what I done — straight. We was drunk or I wouldn't have got married I suppose. We was drinking in them days — make you do anything — if you drink proper way it's different but drink and get larrikin, well there you are (laughter) yeh — well I think it's the truth — larrikin.

My first child from my second husband was in 1945 I

think. Dean was born in 1941. I had to work, cooking. I used to travel up and down with my dad with the camels when I was a girl and learnt cooking then. I used to do dressmaking at school, making this, making that and when I left school that was my living in Oodnadatta — that was dad's home there. In 1928 we came further down south.

He gave the camels to the two boys then — Akbar and Rocky — he retired and settled down. He decided the two boys was old enough take charge of the camels. Few years after there was no work for camels then — the old transport, only trucks and that. The government put out a form to destroy the donkeys, horses and camels. They treat them like they was nothing. Some camels they impound them — pay keep for them — rent like in the common — they had a paddock and they called it the common and some of them call it the pound I think — put them in the pound like here when catch a stray dog and take it out there and put it in the pound — called the common for animals — dogs, horses, camels

Miriam pretending to drink beer for the camera with Naz-meena Khan at Copley, 1953.

and that. That's how camels had no work then see — transport — very few had camels. Aboriginal people got camels. They making good use of them — they get old broken down motor car — take all the engine part off and put a pole in and get a couple of camels — one on each side or two on each side of pole and four wheels — travel around — bun cart they call it. They got all their belongings in it — travel from camp to camp — haul it along, some will just be dragging along.

Well my brothers had camel string — they used to take loading wool and cement to Lyndhurst Siding from Cordillo Downs. Innamincka, Arrabury and around that area. Sometimes South Australia, sometimes south Queensland and in New South Wales. They had to cart three states. From Bourke they used to go to Queensland, Western Australia and Northern Territory. When I was young used to travel with my father. When I went back and everything changed — I thought I was going to see same.

Afghans were prejudiced against Aboriginal people — yet a lot of them married Aboriginal women, but they didn't want their children to learn anything about Aboriginals ways. They wanted them to keep their way — but I used to be stickybeak — that's why I know. Now people come and ask me about Aboriginal things and I can easy answer. Since we got lost and went round and round — from that day my dad used to say 'Learn my girl, learn.' He was glad. I don't know about prejudice though. A lot of white people's ways too they didn't want us to know. Like killing meat. We wasn't allowed to eat meat from the butcher — Afghan slaughtered them themselves — they had to cut the throat. We was that way too we couldn't eat meat without the Afghan killed it — cut its throat. Even bloomin' fish, my brother caught a fish down in the creek and we run back with it — jumpin' you know and cuttin' our hand and we was running back with the fish. 'What you got there, my kid, my children?' We said 'We brought this fish here for you to cut the throat for us.' He said 'It's already cut you see, Lord cut it, angels cut it.' He explained it to us. He said, 'When Abraham had a holy place, it wouldn't stand when he built it up — falls down — built it up — falls down — something or someone come and push it over unless he killed one of his sons. He got his son there, got him put ranja in his eyes, lipstick and rouge pretty and dress him and blindfolded him — took him to this place where he was going to . . . mother was crying, father took this little boy and put him down and blindfolded him and got this knife. Angel replaced boy with lamb, cut with the knife and threw the knife up in the air — no sound, no cry, nothing, just this (gurgling) and he threw this knife it landed in sea — that's how that fish is cut. When he opened his eyes his little boy's standing over there.' — You read that in the Bible too. They kill a lot of lambs for sacrifice — that's in my father's Bible (Koran) and in our Bible (Christian) too. But I can't read it — I've just got memories. I've got Bible talk everywhere here. No Smoking — No Drinking allowed in my place.

Well, Mohammedan religion very strict. My mother was a Lutheran — a Lutheran born — right up 'til she died she was a Lutheran and my dad's a Mohammedan and I used to think well — you know — when I had sense, my mother was a Lutheran — father's Mohammedan and I didn't like to go and follow my mother — leave my father — or follow my father and leave my mother. I used to go to Methodist, when I was a little kid I used to go to Sunday School. All my kid I had christened in Methodist Church. I used to see a lot of Methodists do a little bit dirty work, well that's what I been doing too. I thought, well I've seen this Brethrens here — and I've never seen nothing — been looking all the time — never seen them doing anything wrong — nothing like today — sly ones.

Dean was a big heavy drinker and used his knuckle too — you just said one word and he didn't answer back, he was just into you. He was wild and gambling and so forth and I seen how he changed. You know how he changed? He got locked up one night for no reason at all, just sitting down drunk — asleep — down main street here on corner. He was sitting there drunk waiting for a taxi to come so he could get a taxi to go up home. The police come — policeman was one of his mates too from Marree. He come and pick him up and lock him up. When he woke up in four walls — what am I doing here — four walls. ' What am I doing here — not my place — stone walls.' His mate said, 'I just brought you back here Dean because you was pretty full and you might wander away and get run over by car or something — you didn't do nothing wrong — that's why we brought you here.' Dean went and he never go home — he was frightened to go and face his wife — he went to work — working for the railways then — went to work and then after work he went back home.

'Where you been?' said Rene and he got shamed — went to church two — three times and preaching to other people now. He's mended lot of broken homes up here — white people not black ones — policeman get him to go too — homes that have broken up — patched up a lot of white people. And I thought if he can do that I think I could — that's how I went then — that's ten year ago — last July — ten year ago — 3rd June. I remember that night I went up — I give smoking away — drinking away — gambling away. Dean said I had a carton cigarettes — one cigarette out of it — he put it away from me. He said to Rene 'Did Mum ask for this?' and I said 'No.' 'Oh she must be forgetting she brought a carton today.' I brought it out and I said 'Here, take this away.' I never looked back because I couldn't go without smoke one time — though I could go couple of days without a feed — just that easy I give it away — will-power.

We drank for devilment — that's all. None of them drink just to make them happy — there's not happiness in them. In some people you know it's happy and some people no good — drink — some of them can't control themself — they let themselves go — there's lot of murdering, broken homes and everything goes on with them — lot of them go murdering and things, all through drink, all drunk — drunken people pick up stone, knife, hammer, anything, broken bottle and crack another poor thing with it, all through drink. They wouldn't do that if they wasn't drinking. They let their brains — their minds go — like ashes — that's through drink. What they call — well excuse me I'm going to tell you straight here — you know what my father used to call drink — Devil's Piss — straight out, straight out. You see that in the Bible — straight out.

I've been living in Port Augusta five years last September and in Marree before then fifty two years and in Oodnadatta before that — school age kid. I been cooking in the Marree pub — cooking for shearers. I got all my reference from them — no good for me now reference — can't be able to stand on my legs.

All but one of my babies was born in hospital — I was up and down, up and down out of bed with my daughter. Nearly died with Kenneth and one I lost — I had a blood transfusion with him. Natural birth, nurse she was a really good old woman.

I've helped deliver some babies. It was some kid — I don't know if that boy's still going to school. I nursed a white woman. This woman left it too late and my daughter went over and said 'My mother nursed a couple of women you know.' They called me over — I asked them for this and that. They had to sterilize the things and I brought this little boy into the world and she had four or five kids before and she reckons that's the best birth she had — natural birth see. That boy must be going up 16 too. And then I nursed young Teresa Dodd. Brought her into the world in a motor car — first gate — about nine miles from Marree. Reggie Dodd was driving. Percy was there, old brother-in-law, Doreen Stuart and me. I said 'Get off the road and pull up.' Kid was laying across my legs. She was choked, tied up with cord too. I said 'Pull up,' and they pulled up and I said 'You got scissors or a knife?' 'No,' I said 'You got a string?' 'No,' I said 'There's a bottle there — give us that bottle — break that bottle.' I said 'Bicycle arrived without pump. You got a daughter Percy.' 'What?' I said 'You got a daughter.' 'I can't hear a kid crying.' I said 'Here it is, bicycle without a pump, it's a little girl.' I broke the bottle and cut the cord and told them tear lace off my petticoat to tie it. We travelled all the way down to Leigh Creek and policeman and sister met us halfway and they took the baby and I travelled with mother. They had to take me in the hospital and show me how to do it — you know after-birth and things like that. It's good to learn. I like to learn anything — be a stickybeak and ask people.

Ruth McKenzie

Ruth witnessed her mother's death, caused by her Aboriginal stepfather carrying out a traditional punishment. She was born at Blood's Creek north-east of Oodnadatta and named Molly. Following her mother's death, she was taken by missionaries, renamed Ruth and raised in the Colebrook Childrens' Home in Quorn. Ruth later married an Adnyamathanha man and had thirteen children. Ruth is now a widow and grandmother and lives sometimes in Oodnadatta, Coober Pedy and Port Augusta.

It was Cruel

I was born at Eringa Station in 1919. That's in South Australia just inside the border of Northern Territory. That's where I was born but I grew up at Blood's Creek. That was a place where all the camel teams, the Afghans, had a spell. There was a shop there and that's where my mother, Rosy, was working for the white lady, Mrs Bailes. That's the only place that I know. The camp that I know was there and I was there with my mother until she got burnt. They burnt her because—I'll tell you now.

When I was a little girl, mum used to work for those Bailes people so my step-father took me to this place once, walking, and somehow, I don't know how it was but you know how children look around, I looked like that and I seen a corroboree, see, and that's all. I said 'Look Dad!' He said, 'Yes, but don't look that way. You go on.' In those days we took notice. They told us not to look back — we'd get killed. I took notice.

I went to this place called Federal, not far from Blood's Creek. I got there, I don't know where the old man was. I don't know how I got back to Blood's Creek, but that night, after that, that's how my mother got killed. It was either my father had to die or my mother or myself, see. So Aboriginal way, one of them had to, so, it was my poor mother. It was early hours of the morning and that morning star was shining and I seen what was happening to my mother but being small, I didn't realize what was happening — what they was doing.

They burnt our wurlie we used to live in. That was burnt — that was that day. My mother used to look after goats for the people that was on Blood's Creek. Go out all day and then come back in afternoon and I think I was having a good time because mum used to dig rabbits and that and I used to think it was lovely then to take my little billy-can full of goat's milk and mum used to put

116

that on the hot coals and boil that up for me. Used to let it get cold and I'd have a drink like that.

I remember first our camp got burnt that morning. Mother put the fire and everything out and went across the creek. We looked back later and seen the camp burning and my old step-father told mum to go back and have a look and she wouldn't. I call him father. Mum wouldn't go back and me being small, I said 'I'll run back.' So I run back to where mum put the fire out. It was out. I don't know how that camp caught on fire.

We went that day and afterwards came back and they just made a break, a wind-break — they call it a break. It was winter time I remember — fire burning. Me and my mother slept on one side and old father slept on the other and I don't know if it was Aboriginal way or not but when that morning star came up I saw the old fella stoking the fire and I was on the break side. The break came over like a bit of a wurlie — shelter from the frost. My mother shifted me from under the break side near the fire for me to get the warmth. I was laying there and I seen the old fella stoking the fire. Next thing I seen him walk around. I may as well tell you the truth. He walked around and set alight to the camp.

See I was sleepy and another thing I was small. The camp got on fire so my mother just grabbed me when I was sleeping and just threw me long way out. I woke up and looked around and I seen the place on fire and seen my mother on fire. She couldn't take her clothes and that off. In those days they opened at the back with buttons and had like Chinese necks. She got burnt and I'll always remember how my mother looked. When you get burnt, it's a terrible thing. You blister all over and I always think if I hear of people getting burnt, well, I know it's cruel.

She suffered all day and at night she was still laying down and I remember, being small, I was still annoying her and didn't realize my mother was nearly dead and I wanted to sleep near my mother. The old bloke said 'No' and my mother said 'She can sleep with me' and I slept on her arm that was all blistered up. I must have been young but I can remember. She told me to lay

117

down there and I must have went off to sleep and next morning I found myself up at the house where mum used to work. I got up and walked out to the goat yard. The goats were still in the yard but I seen someone coming and I thought that must be my mother but it wasn't my mother. It was my sister and she said in our language, 'Don't look out for mother. We got no mother.' I still didn't realize.

I was about 6 I think and I didn't take much notice and I was there with these white people. I was there for a couple of days I think and then a wagon came along that used to cart the loading for all the stations, from Macumba Station — Kidmans. All the loadings to take to different stations — camel wagon. My auntie was on it and her husband. That was my stepfather's sister and the old bloke wasn't there but she said to me 'You come here' and I went up to her and they made room there on the wagon and all the stores was there. They made like a little cave I could go in. 'You go in there.'

The little girl was with me — little white girl and auntie said, 'You tell that little girl her mother's calling' and I told her, 'Your Mum's calling.' They said, 'Quick, get in here' and I got in and they put all that loading over it again. I could breathe and that and they said 'Don't talk.' When the little girl came out she said, 'Where's Molly?' (my name's Molly really). My auntie said, 'Went back to the camp. She'll be back later.' So she ran back to her mother and they started off but the old bloke, my old father, he walked on and we must have got to this place called Eringa Station. Not far — about a mile away. They took everything off while I was sitting there looking around.

That's where we stayed until my father decided to come to Oodnadatta — my stepfather. My sister was there too. My sister used to work at Eringa Station and she used to work and supply the food for me. My sister was full-blood. We had one mother. I had one full-blood brother from my mother and one full-blood sister and another half-caste sister like myself but she was killed too in the Aboriginal way. I don't know what for but someone else done wrong. Them days sister was given instead see. She was killed.

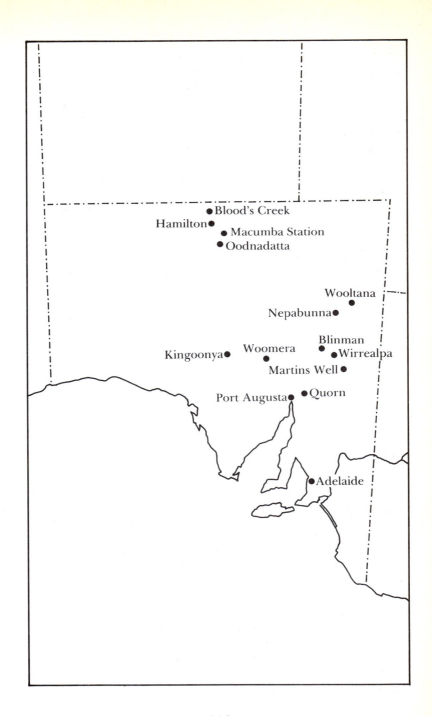

Blood's Creek

Hamilton

Macumba Station

Oodnadatta

Wooltana

Nepabunna

Blinman

Kingoonya

Woomera

Wirrealpa

Martins Well

Port Augusta

Quorn

Adelaide

119

My old father said, 'We'll go to Oodnadatta' — he didn't want to go Blood's Creek way because those people were still after me to take me away to Alice Springs (to the mission home) so we went different way with the wagon but got to this place called Hamilton, old Hamilton. There's a big artesian bore there now. I saw this motor car but they told me, 'If you see a motor car, hide yourself.' I had white hair see. 'Hide yourself because that'll be a policeman and a black tracker.'

I heard the motor car coming and you know being a kid, nosey, looked out from the wagon. Of course the police saw this white hair. They said 'Quick, cover yourself.' Covered myself but it was too late. The police just come and pull the blanket off like that, asked my old father who I was. Mr Virgo his name was, the policeman and the black tracker was Bob Welsh. He told the old fella to go into Macumba Station there. We just camped there one night at this place with auntie, my own auntie. Camped there and next morning when the sun rises, this car pulls up and it was Mr Kemp, Ernie Kemp, from Macumba Station and this quarter-caste bloke, to pick me up.

Them days they didn't come and just say, 'Come on, little girlie' or anything. They just come and got me and put me in the motor car. Of course I jumped out. The old bloke and my relations were hitting themselves (with grief) and I was still crying. I wouldn't stop in the car so Mr Kemp told my auntie 'You'd better come' and when she came I was alright. When I cried for my old step-father, Mr Kemp told me, 'Don't cry. That's not your father because your people's in Oodnadatta.' That was the Lennon's family in Oodnadatta and then I sort of realized I must have been a bit different. I knew I was Aboriginal see.

They took me in to Oodnadatta. Put us in the mission home. There was a lot of other children there. I was there and lonely and one night I ran away with my long nightie and I didn't know where I was but I went to this camp and there was some of my relations. It was George Tongerie's mother. Auntie Nancy we called her and Bob Welsh, the police tracker. I thought I wouldn't wake them up so I went behind the wood heap and went under the wood heap — went to sleep there. I had this long nightie to keep me warm. Next morning I seen the policeman's wife and black tracker looking for me but he knew I was there all the time. So they got this dog see and the dog was tracking me from where I come from. He came straight to the wood heap and stood there. Mrs Virgo looked. I was under there. They got me out and I walked back again — long nightie — being young, small, I wasn't shamed.

We stayed at the home but we wasn't allowed to mix with the full-bloods, the Aboriginal people who washed our clothes and that. We wasn't allowed to go to the camp or anything like that. It got that bad about not wanting us to mix up that they must have made arrangements to shift. They was packing everything up and I remember asking the sister — that's what we called her — Sister Hyde, 'What you packing the clothes up for?' 'Oh,' she said, 'We're going away. Going for a holiday.' I went telling the other kids. They were pleased. The day came that we had to get on the train and Mr Reg Williams was there then and Mr Waye and some of the old people. The Aboriginal people asked me, 'Where you going?' I said, 'We going for a holiday but we'll be coming back.' Long holiday alright. We was brought down to Colebrook Home in Quorn in 1929. I was about 10 year old. I got picked up in 1926.

Them days I went to school in Quorn but we wasn't allowed to talk to any of our relations if they came to Quorn — full-blood ones. We wasn't allowed to talk to them. That was cruel when I was there. I went to grade 4. I could've went higher but the missionaries — they were very cruel to the children. The boys — they used to take their trousers off and give thick straps, lot of straps but they used to pick out the thick ones and they used to belt the boys. This is true, not a lie. Belt the boys, take their trousers off and belt them until they can't cry and that.

When I got a bit older they used to give me a hiding alright. As I got a bit older I thought it was very cruel what they used to do to the boys and to the girls but

121

First children in Colebrook Home, from Oodnadatta.
Ruth is third from left.

when they tried it on me I used to fight the sister back.
Sometimes if I tripped when I'm fighting back, I'd fall
on my stomach. They'd try to sit on me. I used to just
get up and lift them up and fight them back. That's why
they sent me out working early. They thought I was
very naughty but I always think they was too cruel. I
used to tell on them see. I didn't mind if they hit a little
bit but not with big straps. They told me once after I left
the home, 'Ruth, we thought you was like your father
and uncles — the Lennon brothers. They were bad men
and we thought you had taken after them.' They
thought I was going to turn out a terrible girl like them
see.

I worked for Reg Williams at Nepabunna. I don't
know how long — twelve months or so. I used to go back
to the home, up and down, for holidays. Mr Eaton was
the missionary at Nepabunna then but I saw Mr Page
too. I think Mr Page had a nervous breakdown and he
cut his throat but he was a nice chap. He must have had
too much pressure on him and that's what happened.

I met my husband at Reg Williams place. I seen him
there and then went away for a long time and met him
again later. I was only young. I'd never done any
washing or anything in my life because I was going to
school in Colebrook Home and I had to learn to wash
clothes with my hands. In them days, Reg and his wife
were very good to me, very good and after that I came
to Parachilna and there was this German lady, Mrs
Trezona that I was working for. She was the Post
Mistress but she was very, very hard woman. Must have
been about twelve months there. I had to do a lot of
hard work. You know what them big sleepers are, them
heavy sleepers. You mightn't believe it but I had to pick
them up from where they was and carry them to the
wood heap and cut all that up. Fill the wheelbarrow and
stack it away. They had the wood stove them days. Do
that and the housework. Being a German, the floor had
to be real shiny. I had to get down on my knees them
days — nothing like what they got now — and polish it.
She used to stand back and look to see if there was a
scratch. It was that hard and I used to get hot. She was a

very hard woman, that German woman.

I was working there for a long time and Mr Fargo, he was the station owner from Blinman, he came there once to the Post Office and he seen me how I was working and he felt sorry for me. He thought, 'She's a good girl.' So, I suppose he found out where I come from and he wrote away to the mission. In those days you were under the Aboriginal Protector — Chief Protector. Mr Fargo said he thought I was a good girl and he'd like to have me so they wrote up and said I could go there.

Well, they were different. Mr and Mrs Fargo of Oratunga Station. It was four miles out from Blinman. They were different people, different altogether. I don't know how the German people felt about that. I was only too glad to go when Mr Fargo came and got me away from there. I used to do everything — all the housework. Mrs Fargo used to do all the cooking and things. I was there I think about three years. I didn't have to pay rent or nothing. They thought the world of me because I was a good girl. I used to do everything right because they treated me different. Fargo's treated me different therefore I did more work, see? Well, I did my work for Mrs Trezona too but she was hard.

I got paid but it wasn't much. They had to put some money into the bank but we never seen that money. There was only me working at Blinman. I think I was the only girl. The others from Nepabunna weren't working and that's where I learnt everything. I picked up everything.

I got married after that in the Colebrook Home. My white relations didn't want me to. They didn't want me to marry an Aborigine, you know to go back to Aborigines, but I remember telling them 'I'll marry him. He's the same colour as myself.' I married him, the person that I want — same colour as myself and I married him. Emily Lester was my bridesmaid. She's around here now. I was married the Christian way. I had to get permission from the Chief Protector to marry my husband. It was hard for us to marry Aboriginal — I don't know what for. I think they wanted to keep us away

124

from our people but I remembered my sister and I remembered my brother. I never forgot them and they were good to me and that's why I'll never forget my people.

I remember my brother going through on the train. Some men had been in jail for killing bullocks. One was my brother and that's how I got caught. Mr Virgo, the policeman and the police tracker was going out Hamilton way to track these Aborigines that killed the bullock and my brother was one of them. He was in Port Augusta jail. I don't know how long he was there. That was in 1929 and that's when Sister Hyde wouldn't even let me talk to him because he was black and he had to stand away. Aborigine fella came up to me and told me but I knew it was my brother and he couldn't come. All I could do was wave and that was the last time I ever seen him. They came up to see me because they knew I was in Quorn but the missionaries wouldn't let me talk to him. He came to see me after he got out of jail. The train was staying in Quorn for a few hours — the Ghan I think.

I never forgot my name. I used to be Molly Lennon but the missionaries changed it to Ruth Selha, from the Bible. It's a good thing I never forgot my name. I remember one time they lied to some Jewish people. It was Reg Williams in Quorn. He used to go to Adelaide now and again and he knew some Jewish people who was well off. This was at the meal table and we was all sitting there and he told them that I was a Jew — part Aborigine, part Jew. I never said nothing but I thought I know what I am. I'm a Lennon. These people wanted to take me and they asked me would I like to be adopted. I'd have everything. I'd go to high school but in my mind — I had my sister in my mind and my brother. I said, 'No, I don't want to be adopted.' It was a terrible thing for those people to think I was a Jew and I wasn't. So that was it — he couldn't do nothing.

One time I seen my white father. I forgot to tell you before. When mum died he came to Blood's Creek. I could have seen him before that but I can't remember. See my father, my Aboriginal father, was a jealous man.

125

He had a lot of wives and that's why I wasn't allowed to see my real father but I seen him after my mother died although he didn't know my mother died. He'd come to see her. I think it was him that went and told these white people to take me.

When I married and had children we worked around stations sometimes around Roxby Downs. During the war it must have been and a lot of soldiers were going through there — through the rocket range — Woomera and that and surveyors were there too. Len Beadell took photos of us. He took a photo of the daughter that I lost. She was 4 years old. I didn't have a photo of my daughter and one day I was looking through this book in a shop in Port Augusta and I thought I knew that face. I didn't take much notice then went back and had a good look. It was Angelina, my eldest and my other daughter that I lost. It was him that took that photo so I've got it now.

That was a cruel thing when I was in Nepabunna. See my husband was from there but I was from up north. I was an outsider and in the Aboriginal way the children are classed on the mother's side. You come from the mother and therefore you're that tribe and my daughter was real sick and I didn't know what was wrong but I knew she was real ill. My in-laws wouldn't even help me to bring the body back to Nepabunna from Adelaide and I couldn't get down there because I just had a baby. Molly had a tumour. She fell off the tree, fell off the shed and hit her head and we left it and it turned into a tumour. Not long ago I went to Adelaide and I went to the cemetery. I knew where she was buried and found her grave. She died in 1939. That was the cemetery on West Terrace. It was a government burial them days. That was that. I couldn't even get down to her funeral or anything. I tell you I had hatred for the Adnyama-thanha tribe and I have got it still but I suppose because I'm a Christian I forgive them — my in-laws. I talk to them and that but I'm always thinking. They thought Molly had a disease.

My husband told me that the full-bloods before he come were bigger people. They were tall and big. They

Molly and Angelina McKenzie at Roxby Downs, 1948.
This is Ruth's only photo of her daughter Molly who died soon
after following a fall.
Photo by Len Beadell.

had everything them days, native foods, but they got mixed up, in-bred, different now.

He told us stories. Leigh Creek must have been scrub. It must have been jungle. That's what my husband said. All this country was jungle. That's a long way back and there used to be big snakes but the seasons changed. Drought and that came and buried everything up and what they call Yandama sandhills the other side of lake Frome — all those sandhills — that's all the trees that's covered up. I think they've found animals there. Animals were bigger — wombat, kangaroo. Everything was a lot larger than what they are now. That's what he said. Australia was different from what it is now, like it's all barren country now. It was like Darwin I suppose. Everything's changed now.

I know Wilpena going to Martin's Well there's some sort of cave. You go in the hole and come out and Martin's Well there but they reckon that the snake, the Adnyamathanha's call it akurra, used to go in there. That snake used to live around. I don't know if you know it but they reckon that those big Nullabor holes — caves — that's wanambi in my language — that's a big snake — their hole. My husband wanted to leave his stories but he said the children aren't bothering. I'll die with all my secret stories. He wanted it for all the children that's coming up.

It kept children in their place when they had their own law. The men weren't allowed to mix up with young girls. They had to camp further away from the girls and the brothers wasn't allowed to come near the sister. The sister would cook meals, that's what I seen and get everything ready. The sister would walk away and the brothers would come into that place and get their meals. Everything's changed. They've all got their different ways.

Eva Strangways

Eva's parents were Antikirinja and Kookatha and she grew up with her extended family mostly along the Transcontinental railway line, travelling around pastoral stations with camel wagons undertaking casual work. Later she lived with her several children and grandchildren in the opal mining town of Andamooka in a two roomed tin shack with no power or running water. Eva is now a grandmother and lives in Port Augusta.

Travelling the Stations

Do you know Tarcoola? I was born at Immarna Siding where they make this new (railway) siding through, that's the time I'm born there. It's a siding this side of Ooldea. Immarna, then Barton, Wynbring, Tarcoola then. That's in 1917. I was born out in the bush I suppose. No hospitals and stuff. My father's half-caste and mother's a full Antikirinja. My father's Kookatha, so I'm half and half I suppose. My name was Egan. Father's Ted Egan and mother's Ruby Egan.

We used to live in Wilgena, Tarcoola and all them (pastoral) stations. My father worked stations. Come back this way then, Kingoonya, Roxby, Purple Downs and all them. That's because my father used to do sheep work, mustering, riding horses. We travelled around with camels, string of camels. We had saddles on the camels. We weren't frightened — used to it. We walked along first — we'd get tired — have a ride.

We had two children in the family. Brother was in another place. There was my father, mother and some other people. Lots of people. My father was head stockman. Some worked other stations. I didn't know the station owners. We had no house, just a humpy with canvas. Some had tents. We didn't ever play with the white kids from the station. We used to have a game, rounders, like baseball. We call it rounders. All kids play, all day too. We had a board, not a proper bat. Mans used to play too, some of the womans join in with the kids. We ate damper and meat — tinned meats and vegetables. Got them off the train.

We had bush tucker, plenty wild peaches and some little berries. I don't know what they call it. Lot of things but I can't know the name. We made flour, got seeds and grind them up. Big bush, they get the seed off, put it on the big rock and grind it. My mother did that. She had tin dishes. That was when I was little. Used to catch kangaroo with kangaroo dog. They chase them and catch 'em. Father had a rifle. We'd dig rabbits out too and shoot them or kill them with the stick. Sometimes cook them in the ashes, sometimes in the pot. Had plenty meat.

The old people made spears and boomerangs. A lot of old people done that, boomerangs and waddies and all them things. Made them to sell along the railway line. My old grandmother was telling me they used to sell the boomerangs and that and the people give them some money, sovereigns, all the silvers to buy the things. They used to dig a hole and bury the money up, all the moneys. It could be still there in the sandhills. They don't know it's money. Some black peoples come from up that way. Some white peoples tell them that's money to buy tucker, but they take it and dig a hole and bury them up.

The railway went out to Ooldea and come back this way again carting food and everything. When they see that coming, they *take off*. They run away frightened. They think it's the devil coming. They went over the sandhills, go away and come back, they don't know. They think it's mamu. That's when they putting in the railway first, see. Willy Austin's mother was telling me about those things. I must have been a baby I suppose.

When I was little I used to go to the inmas. We'd see the dances, the man's and the woman's, everyone. Sometimes we danced. We're too shamed to teach our children.

When we was kids we just played. There was no school — school was in Tarcoola. There was two missionaries, Miss Brown and Miss Lock. They was in Ooldea where they had a mission. We was in the pastoral stations see. They wouldn't keep us in the mission because we're everywhere going. Some people lived in the mission but our fathers, they got to work, you know, take us away.

We didn't ride on the trains, not that days. Train was going but we're at the station all the time. We met Miss Lock when she was going through. That was in Coon-

131

dambo Station, this side Kingoonya. Didn't meet Daisy Bates, she was in Ooldea all the time. Never went that far. Heard people talking about her. She used to stay there when the people come from the outback, when they come with no clothes on. She got clothes there — give them clothes. When they want to come into the town, Tarcoola, they'll have clothes.

We travelled around until I got big I suppose. We met Miss Brown, she was another missionary. Miss Brown used to teach us in Tarcoola. We'd sit there when my father had no work. They sent us to the lady missionary. She taught us Gospel. I wanted to stay there (but our parents) they had to take us away again. When they go for work, we have to go.

We stayed just around there, Kingoonya, just around there. I must have been growing up just around that little area. When I grow up we come up this way then to Andamooka. I looked after Max Thomas (now a Kookatha elder). His mother got a lot of children. Lorna Sultan asked me to look after one little boy. I was 14 then, big girl. He was about 3, might have been 4, I suppose. I had to look after him. We was always travelling around there.

Come from Coondambo to Andamooka, Roxby, went to Andamooka then. He stayed with us a couple of years and we left him there then with his mother at Andamooka. He's an old man now. He wants to get our land back but he can't get it. Probably we can't get it back.

We went up this way then to Iron Knob then around there and went back up. Just travelling. That's alright that time. Back to Kingoonya, then back to Tarcoola. That's what my parents was doing. They had Aboriginal business (initiations, men's business), their business, that's what they was doing, going up and down with other people, back to their own camps. I didn't have a promised husband. I could pick any, anyone you like. I've had nine children, four daughters, four sons and one I lost. When I had my first one, must be about nineteen or older, not like this life now. They having 'em when they're girls. Mine were born in the bush with another lady to help.

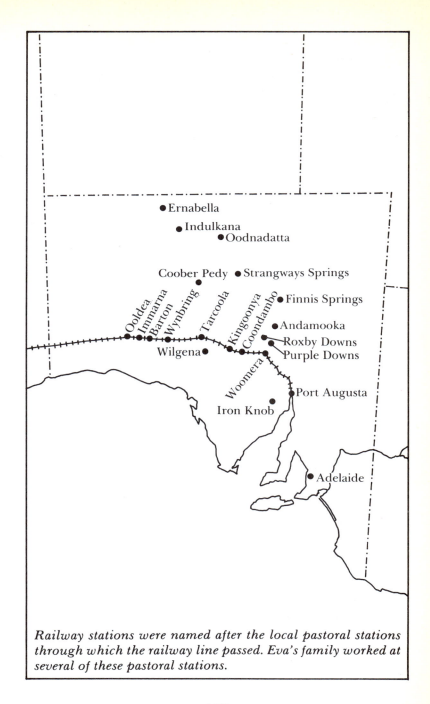

Railway stations were named after the local pastoral stations through which the railway line passed. Eva's family worked at several of these pastoral stations.

133

I knew Milly Taylor then. Milly came from Ernabella to Coober Pedy. Met her in Kingoonya there and all them people. A lot of people was there in Woomera just for the day. Went there from Andamooka opal field. We was living at the opal field for sixteen years. We went into Woomera. Come past there to get to Port Augusta. Got to go past there. There was a hospital there. They took us in there for needle but don't know what that's for? They took us in big trucks, truckloads.

I know old MacDougall, he was staying there too. He used to go and get the people too and take them to the hospital. I met him in Woomera. He used to be up Oodnadatta way and when that Woomera started, he was there then. When anybody sick, he used to go and get the people and take them to the hospital.

I remember the bombs going off. We was in Andamooka there living. We heard about it. A lot of people got sick there, all around that way. Could be because of that (bomb tests).

We found opals in old days. Get some in the dumps. Buyers buy it. That's how we used to live there. No pension that time. We got good price. Got some opal and buy some food. We got $100 or $40 that time. They don't make dug-outs like Coober Pedy, not much hills there. Houses were holes in the ground with roofs over them, not dug into sides of hills. We had sort of a shack, good enough to live. The government made it for all the peoples everywhere, little houses. Our kids went to school there. All my grandsons and three of mine.

The house had two rooms, no pipes for water, just a house. People cart water on big trucks in drums. We had lights, carbide light they call it. It was light to go down for the opal. Good lights too, like Tilley lights, just like that. Sometimes you get a candle when things run out. We had to buy all our own blankets and mattresses and that. Get a lot of food up there. We had lots of people in the house. Piled up, there's some in the kitchen — kids in the kitchen. Kids and some grandchildren. We had a tub to wash clothes, no machine, no washing board. Boil a bucket, drum, you know make a bucket out of it. We had a stove, wood stove and kerosene fridge. Opal miners used kerosene ones too, gas too. We was good friends with white people, Yugoslav, all them peoples. They was good friends.

My husband's Tim Strangways. He worked on the stations too. Strangways come from Finnis Springs. There's Finnis Springs, Strangways Springs. That's my husband's name. His people are Arabana. His mother is Kujani. My kids are mixed up. They'll be four — Antikirinja, Kookatha, Arabana and Kujani. My husband been gone a long time. My children went to Andamooka school and school at the stations. My children are Johnny Strangways, the eldest (he's gone now), lost one, his name was Leo, Thelma, Cathy, Cyril, Brian, Eileen and Lynette. My brother was Scotty Egan. He's gone now. He was sick, too much drink, like the rest and my father's gone. He was old then, got sick.

I got married firestick way, not the Christian way. We went up to Finnis Springs, my husband's country, when we had my father's camels. We all used to travel around with the camel buggies. A bit later my father had a trolley, trailer for two camels when we was working on stations then. I got one picture in my room, my father sitting on the horse. We travelled around. My parents were gone before we got christened. They're buried here in Port Augusta — cemetery up here. I still go to church now.

We had to bring the kids down here to Port Augusta when they're big for high school. They got one in Andamooka now. We lived at the Davenport reserve until we got a place here in town. I moved back to my daughter Eileen there. Had to go back there. Lynette is my youngest with the babies, must be about 20 I suppose, or about 25. I had my babies out in the bush. We weren't frightened. Just put up with it. Clean them up in the sand. All my babies are bush babies.

I used to talk to my husband in English. I can't talk his language, Arabana. My parents talked some English, some words. I just learnt a bit. We talked in our language. My kids know our language too, Antikirinja.

There were some places we weren't allowed to go when I was little. A long time ago, not allowed to go, old

135

people used to be very strict. If we go and play around there, we'd get killed. That's how we don't know much about the sites. Only old people could go there. There's one women's place at Andamooka. Only women allowed to go there. I know the seven sisters (Dreaming) story, you might already know, a lot of people talk about it. People (up north) still travelling around, they know a bit. My sons are too frightened to go up that way. Kookatha's traditional life all gone now.

I've travelled to a lot of places now, Indulkana and Ernabella. I went with the Brethren church in a bus with my grandson, just for a holiday. I've been to Melbourne, Thelma and Kathy's in Melbourne and Brian, my son's in Brisbane. They're all over the place. Two live with me, Eileen and Lynette.

I've been to Adelaide after I had all my kids. It was alright. I was in hospital there for months for my eyes. Lash was growing in, scratching 'em, making it bleed. I was glad to get better. My eyes were bad for a long time, must be about five years, I suppose. Doctor from Port Augusta sent me. When people got sick before, they just get better themselves. Some people used to go into Woomera, tell the doctor, get some tablets. Some go on the Flying Doctor plane. Doctor goes to the camp and gives medicine. We had our doctors and medicines too. Mix bush with tea leaf — drink it for colds, flu.

Young fellas used to play guitar, play Slim Dusty, all them songs. No drink that time, they never drink. Just lately they're drinking. The old people was strict. You'd get a big hiding.

I've been to the 'Bubbler' (artesian spring) near Finnis Springs. Only the Kujani people can talk. My old mother-in-law told me. She took me there to show me. It brings dry sand up then water, full again and bubbles. That thing floating around, that stopped in the water. You seen the hair on a horse, behind the neck — (it's) something like that. They reckon it's got hair, that big snake. Something made it blind before a long time ago.

I've been to Strangways Springs too. Been all around there, just going in a car. They reckon people put a pipe there, to reach the bottom. Something sent the pipes up

Eva's family group at Coondambo, 1948.
Ruby (Eva's mother) is sitting at left. Eva is on the left of the group and her father Ted Egan is in the centre.
Photo by Len Beadell.

Eva's family at East Well, Coondambo, 1948, with their camel wagon. Eva's husband, Tim Strangways is holding the horse in front. Ruby, her mother, is at the left of the camel.

when they poke them, pushes them out. That old lady used to tell me. That fella went back and died. He went back to go to sleep and he was finished in the morning, dead. They tried to put bolts, tried to shut that up, make a tank. Next morning he was dead.

I helped women have babies. I helped Milly Taylor. Just cut the cord, tie a knot, put a nappy around, sort of a bandage and keep dry. We watch it, see what they're doing to us and you do it to others. Mother rests about five or six days. Sometimes it's hard, got to struggle, nothing for pain. No men's allowed to go. After about five days the mother might go back to the camp. Takes a couple of days for the baby to go brown. We'd just keep having babies, can't stop them.

Milly Taylor

Milly's Aboriginal mother and Irish father and their children travelled around the north-west and through to Oodnadatta with a camel team delivering rations and collecting dingo scalps. Later Milly's mother settled at Ernabella near the mission but left after a year feeling homesick for her people and country. They travelled across country living a traditional lifestyle, hunting and gathering traditional foods to survive. Still later, they were exploited by some station owners but then found kind people at another station. Milly has had many children and grand-children and lived for many years in Port Augusta, returned to the northwest and Alice Springs and has since settled in Coober Pedy where she cares for her family and works with her people.

Born Out Bush

I was born in the bush at a place called Wallatinna near Indulkana. There were no hospitals then. In my family are seven, myself, three sisters and three brothers. We were all born out bush. There's Bill, born at Opposite Creek just behind Ernabella: Barney, born at Wallatinna; Clem, born at Evelyn Downs, he's finished now though. Then there's Tilly, born at Welbourn Hill near Coober Pedy; Emily, born at Apara near Amata and Dorothy, born at Ernabella just behind the new hospital between the rocks.

Our mother was a full blooded Antikirinya woman, named Molly. My father was an Irish man, Jim Lennon and he was a real good father to us all.

My father had twelve camels and two horses. The camels were given to him by the government so that he could go out then and kill the dingos for their scalps, then send the scalps down south by train. Then they would send supplies back to him so he could take everything out to all the Aboriginals that lived at Apara, Puta-Puta and all them places. The Aboriginals then were real wild people. They had no clothes, until my father gave out to them everything they needed, clothes, flour, tea and sugar.

They didn't know anything about the mixing of the flour or how to make damper, and they didn't even know how to make tea until my father and mother talked to them and showed them how to. After that they became real friendly with my father and mother, and then they used to help him find the dingo pups. They had to dig them out of the holes, knock them on the head, then scalp them, take them back to the camp, dry them out, then put ashes through the scalps so that they didn't smell. They also did that to the dingos' tails and ears as well. Then my father would go back to Oodnadatta to pick up more supplies and take it back out to the Aboriginal camps, they would have all the dingo scalps ready waiting for him.

I suppose they trusted my father to get more food and clothing for them. That's why they worked so hard to get as many dingo scalps as they could. When the other white fellas would go to the Aboriginal camps and try to get scalps off them, they would lie and say they got nothing. They would hide them away, until my father got there and give them to him, so that he could get more supplies for them. They really trusted him more than the others because some of them were real cruel. They would take the scalps and just give them one stick of tobacco or offer the father and mother clothes for a young girl. That's why they used to run away whenever they saw a white man, only for my father they came to know the white people today cause he showed them he was a good man. They still talk about him today. The Aboriginals gave my father an Aboriginal name, Katiti, which meant buck tooth.

When we were moving around on the camels, we stopped every afternoon for a sleep. One day when we were little; we played around while my parents slept and later that day we got really tired when we were back on the camels and fell asleep and my sister Tilly fell off the camel.

My father used to make a big wind break for us to sleep in but if it was raining he would put up a tent. My father, mother and big brother had a rifle each just in case we had any trouble. He didn't have to use it on anyone. It was just to protect us and for hunting because we had a lot of wild meat, like euros, kangaroos and wallabies.

After that my father had a place called Opposite Creek. That's when we started to settle down. We had sheep, horses and some goats. When we first moved to Opposite Creek my father built a house of mud and grass put together. He also started a vegetable garden for us. Then he got a horse and buggy to go into Ernabella to get the mail. We still had the camels with us. I think we lived there for about two or three years. Some of the Aboriginals were working for my father. They used to shepherd the sheep and the goats. They used to get three meals a day and were looked after properly by my parents.

My cousin, Ruby Woods' husband, Stanley Ferguson, built a house in Ernabella out of the same materials that my father used and they lived there for a very long time and had one son called Donald Ferguson. Donald's parents are finished now, and he lives in Alice Springs with his own family. Stanley had sheep, goats and horses as well. That's when the government people started to push the white people out of Ernabella and make a Presbyterian Church there. The first missionaries in Ernabella were Mr and Mrs Taylor and the first school teacher was Mr Trudinger. He used to teach all the half-caste kids English and the other Aboriginal kids Pitjantjatjara.

I went to church there with the missionaries. Then Mr and Mrs Taylor asked me to go and have Christmas in Melbourne with them, so I said 'Yes, I'd love to come.' On our way to Melbourne we camped at Bookaloo. When we were asleep I heard this big noise sounded like a big wind, then I started screaming. Mr Taylor jumped up and said 'What's the matter, that's only a train going by,' so then we all sat up and watched the train pass by. When we got to Melbourne we had Christmas there. That's when Mrs Taylor got sick and went into hospital so we stayed for a while with Mr Taylor's sister at her place.

I helped look after Ann who was five and Marjorie who was three. Their grandma used to come and pick us up and take us for a ride on the trams, it was my first time. They were real nice christian people. That's the time Mr MacDougall took over. Mr Taylor asked me if I wanted to go back to Ernabella with Mr MacDougall or did I want to stay with them. I said I'd like to stay and help him with the two little ones but I can't because I want to go back and see my mother, brothers and sisters.

That's when the welfares and police came to Ernabella and grabbed all the half-caste kids, chucked them on the mail truck and sent them to Oodnadatta. From there they were put on the train and sent on down south. That's why some of the half-caste people today don't even know where they were born or who their real family were. Lois O'Donoghue can help find out who their real family is because she met her own mother when she was a grown woman herself, that's why she tries to help people as much as she can. Lois's parents owned a station called Kantja. They were a happy family, they were well dressed people, until her father went to World War Two and he didn't return. Then Lois' Uncle Nganngi (which means fat frog) looked after them all at the station when his brother died. Nganngi was a real good old bloke. He used to work real hard to look after the place and the kids. That's when our own family was split up. My father took us into Ernabella and told us that we had to stay in the mission there because he was told that he couldn't have an Aboriginal woman cause he wasn't legally married to her. So he went away from Ernabella because he was kicked out of there. He told the welfares that he didn't want his kids to be sent down south that they had to stay with their own mother and go to school in Ernabella. So we stayed in Ernabella and my father went down to Coober Pedy.

I just went to pieces because my parents were no longer living together. I didn't want to go to school any more because it wasn't the same without dad. If we still had dad with us then I probably would have gone to school and learnt to read and write. I really loved my father and mother and I didn't want to see them sort of things happening to them. After that my mother used to work very hard to try and keep my brothers and sisters going. She used to do gardening, wash dishes and stuff like that at the mission home. I was the only one going to school then, and I think she found it very tough not having anyone else to help her with the kids. My mum used to go to the prayer meetings at six o'clock every morning before she started work. That's why I used to get real sorry for my mum whenever I saw her working. I wasn't real happy at all. I worried about my father — that's why I think I used to run away from school.

I used to run away from school all the time. When you run away from school, you'd get a hiding but next day I

143

Children at Ernabella School, 1940.
Albert Lennon at far right, Milly's nephew.
Mountford-Sheard Collection in State Library of SA.

Ron Trudinger, teacher at Ernabella in classroom with children. Children's names are listed on blackboard headed by Milly and Tilly, sisters who are now Milly Taylor and Tilly Waye from Port Augusta.

Mountford-Sheard Collection in State Library of SA.

used to take off again and I'd come back and get another hiding and run away again, for about a week or two weeks. When I'd get hungry I'd go back — for a feed. I'd run away down in the bush.

When I was in the home we got clothes and the dark ones weren't allowed to have clothes. They had to run around naked. I was the silliest one there I think, I used to run away with all the kids and take my clothes off and go home naked because I'd look funny, only one got clothes, everyone else has got nothing.

My father used to get clothes for us, but when I was in the home there, only half-caste kids used to have clothes and all the dark ones go without clothes when they started school. It was cold too winter time. They had sort of a big waterhole there on the side of Ernabella in the creek. It was a spring running all the time and everyone had to have a shower in the morning. All the kids had to line up and dive in that water and come out other side and no towels. They had to run around until they got warm.

They used to make a fire to get warm and the teacher used to come along with a whip. They had a whip and chased kids away from that fire with the whip. That was Mr Trudinger. I don't know if he's dead or not. He went back to America. They got a film of that time — the people in Ernabella. When I went up there about four years ago, they showed me it. Only about one year I went to school. That's why I can't read and write.

We was at the mission home for about two years, that's when my mother must have been missing my dad because she wanted to go away, so she told me she wanted to go to Hamilton to see her mother and brother, that's all she had, so we just packed our stuff and went to Hamilton. Mum's father was Pitjantjatjara and her mum was half Antikirinya, half Aranda. We walked around to Kulgera, from there we went to Indulkana. That's when we used to eat bush tucker like rabbits, witchettys and wangunu, it's like wheat, you have to grind it with a rock to make flour, also wakati and iluwa, it's the same as wangunu, you use them to make flour too, they grow like wheat but on shorter bushes. You don't see much around now. Our mother taught us how to use the grinding stones. I don't really like the taste of wangunu but I had to eat it or starve. We had blankets for a little while then when they were worn out we slept without them. Clothes wore out too. We were naked all the time. There was a big mob of us. We had inmas. They had women's business too to teach us what to do and dances. Men were not allowed to see them.

Mum would get up in the morning and pray before she'd go out and get some food for us. She'd come home with a lot of things, rabbits, witchettys, kumpurarpa — tastes like a lemon but sort of sweet — they grow in little bushes and they're yellow. It's really nice — we used to eat that all the time. You're not allowed to eat too much or you'll get sick in the tummy — they give you just enough to eat and if you want more — they wouldn't give it to you. They'd give you something else, bit of meat.

We might get one kangaroo or euro. They would cook it up and share that kangaroo — everybody's got to have a piece — if it's only a mouthful, its still got to go around. Not allowed to be greedy and have too much — all the kids got to have just a little bit each.

All the kids used to go up in the hills and make noise and the kangaroos or euros would rush down to the ground — the men wait and get them with spears — emus, kangaroos, goannas, perenti, wallaby, euro, turkey and a little thing — we used to call mala. They go down in the hole and when they dig they go straight down, down and down real deep. They used to still dig that up to eat.

They used to have itjari-itjari, it's real flat but got different lips and they used to chase that around and it used to dig a hole real fast — they dig *real* fast — they can't catch it. They got to wait until they come out and get them then and kill it. If you dig — you can sit there all day and dig for it — it's going real fast.

After that my mum sort of broke away from the mob and she had two girls and one bloke who helped her with us to Indulkana. We had a ride with the camel wagon to a place called Kantja. Don't know what whitefellas used to call it — its between Indulkana and Kulgera.

After that we went to Lambina and we stayed in Lambina for a month. There was some of my mother's relations there. Then after that we walked from Lambina to Todmorden, then my mother got a job there, shepherding goats. The lady that used to own the station wanted me to go to school there and she used to teach me now and again, but I didn't like it, I only wanted to go sometimes. When I think about it today, I feel real stupid for not going and learning. From Todmorden we went on to Hamilton and soon as we got there we found out that my grandma had passed on, she passed on about two weeks before we got there, but my mum's brother Jack was still there. After about five years he passed on too. So we hurried around and went back to Todmorden and stayed there for a while with mum's cousin.

Mum got the job back and she worked there for a while and after that we left. We went to Oodnadatta and she got another job there so we stayed there for about a couple of months. Mum worked in the store at Oodnadatta, helping until these white people from Evelyn Downs Station came looking for someone to work for them, so then mum got the job at Evelyn Station which is near Coober Pedy. We were real slaves there. I used to chop wood, and wash clothes by hand in a big tub with just soap and water, then hang them on the line, then this old lady used to go and grab all the clothes off the line and throw it back into the tub and say now wash it properly, they are not clean. So I used to wash it over again and it was still not good enough for her. Then I used to take off down the creek and climb the big trees so that the dogs couldn't get me. They used to look everywhere for me. When they turned around and went back home I used to climb down off the tree and run to where my mum was working at the sheep camp which was about two miles away from the homestead. I used to sleep there for one night but they would come in the morning and take me back and give me a new job.

148

They taught me how to skin the sheep and cut up the sheep meat. After a while I became like a butcher, and got used to the hard work. I used to cook bread for all the workers, but still I didn't like the idea of my little brothers and sisters working. They used to shepherd sheep and goats. They had to get up real early to milk the goats and then take them out and look after them. It was winter time then, they used to cry whenever they went into the goat yard because their little feet would get wet and freezing. They used to give us an alarm clock and set it up for five o'clock. Whenever the alarm clock went off some of us would jump up and the little ones would start crying and I would tell them don't cry, I can't help it, we have to go and work you know.

They didn't pay us much. They used to give us one dress every month, nothing else, just a dress. No jumper — no shoes, nothing. No underwear, no blankets, we used to sleep under bags. We couldn't go anywhere. We didn't know where we was. It was near Coober Pedy, that's rough country that is.

We got sick of it, so we ran away and ended up in Mabel Creek. Me and my sister, Tilly, got a job there, but my mother didn't stay with us. She took the three younger children with her, then me and Tilly learnt to look after ourselves and earn our own money. It was really good there. We got paid and got a lot to eat. We got blankets, mattress, everything.

Mum was also earning money by digging opals at Coober Pedy. That's when we met up with dad and my big brother again. We were real glad to see them. We used to see them quite often after that. My father was getting very old then, but he still tried to help mum by digging opal with a pick and shovel. My oldest brother took Bill and tried to look after him but he didn't like it there because I think he didn't know them that well. They left when he was a little boy.

They were living in a very small dugout and that's when the welfares came from Port Augusta looking for some more half-caste kids. They came and talked to mum about the kids. My mother wasn't sure whether to let them go, but I had to talk with her, and said 'Let them go mum, they won't be far, we can go and visit them, and they can learn to read and write.' Mum said yes, she started crying, then my little sister said 'Don't cry mum, when I learn to read and write I'll come back and teach you.' So they took them into Kingoonya and Miss Morton was there waiting for them. There was four little half-caste kids, my brother Bill and sister's Emily, Dorothy and Henry O'Toole, he was the wildest one there, he tried to jump out of the train window, I heard. So after that we used to go by train and visit them all the time. They were happy in the home.

I met Harry Taylor in Mabel Creek and we got married at the Port Augusta Mission. We had two sons, Samuel and Malcolm and one daughter, her name was Shirley but she passed away when she was a baby. Samuel was born in Evelyn Downs, Malcolm was born in Wirraminna and then Shirley was born at Eight Mile just out of Coober Pedy. I lived with Harry for about five years, then he left me and went back to Alice Springs. Then I started working in Wirraminna Station for Mr and Mrs Jenkins, they were nice people. After that when I used to get sick of working I used to travel around with my mother and all the other old people. I reckon it's with that atomic bomb that everyone got sick in Wirraminna there because my mum got real sick there too and my kids. I reckon that was the first testing of the bombs, see we was there before the other Aboriginal people came along, there was the Egan's, Strangway's and our family.

We used to go to this big rock-hole called Koolymilka, but now it is a very sacred place for the white people. I don't know why, but before that it was a free country. I don't know whether it's still the same. They used to move us when they started shooting rockets to Parakylia there somewhere. They used to go and talk to the old peoples — my mum was still living then and we had these old peoples — Eva Strangways' old father and Egan. When we used to come in shopping to Woomera we used to have a lot of trouble. Police used to pick us up and take us up into the police station but Mac-Dougall, who I knew from Ernabella, he was working

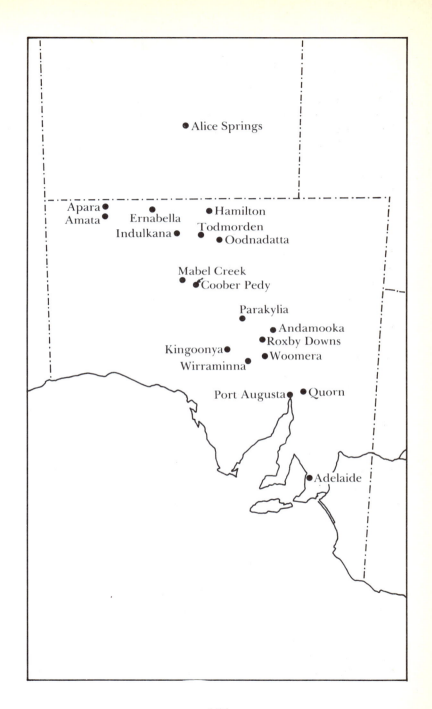

● Alice Springs

Apara ●
Amata ●   ● Hamilton
        Ernabella
Indulkana ●   Todmorden
              ● Oodnadatta

    Mabel Creek
        ● ●Coober Pedy

            Parakylia
            ●
                ● Andamooka
                ●Roxby Downs
    Kingoonya●
            ●Woomera
    Wirraminna●

    Port Augusta● ● Quorn

            ●Adelaide

151

there and he helped a lot of blackfellas there in Woomera. I don't know why they picked us up.

MacDougall would talk to Egan and he'd tell us then 'We gotta move out of here today, or tomorrow, because they gotta send off rockets and things like that.' See that time they used to shoot rockets and move us back to Wirraminna — got to keep on that side — until they shoot these rockets off — some place.

That bomb shook the ground. It's sort of a funny smell too, just like smoke, funny sky — like a dust storm and we didn't even know where that thing went off see — it shook the ground and frightened everybody.

You know MacDougall got kicked out from there because he was helping too many peoples there. They was going to jail him. He come and told us. In Wirraminna, he is the one who used to rush out and let everyone know. 'They'll be sending rockets and shooting bomb.' He really liked dark people.

When everyone gets sick they went to the hospital in Woomera. My kids been in hospital there. One little boy died there — he was born with TB I think. That was Johnny Strangways little son — he was only a little baby. He used to lay down and make a noise, making a funny noise when he's sleeping.

Everyone got sick there. Mr Jenkins, the owner of the station, died with cancer.

Before, when we was kids, not even my brothers and sisters got sick. Every time we'd catch cold or something, my father used to give us one drop of eucalyptus in the sugar and we used to drink that. We'd take a long time to take that too. He tied us up under the tree and told us 'Take that eucalyptus.' And when it's getting dark he'd say 'Sleep there tonight if you're not going to take the medicine — sleep there — no blanket.' We'd say, 'We'll take the medicine then.' Start to get frightened in the dark. That's all we used to take. There's a drop of eucalyptus on the pillow if we got blocked nose — that's all we had — blocked nose and a sort of a sore throat when you had a cold. Never got real sick.

My mum got real sick. She was a real strong woman. In Coober Pedy, she used to dig some opal out with a crowbar. She used to get a lot of opal out with a crowbar.

My other kids were born in Port Augusta, they haven't been sick like the first ones. They're real healthy kids. Only the first ones that was born around Woomera and Wirraminna. Food, we had everything, used to get vegetables off the train that used to go through. Fresh apples, oranges, tomatoes, pumpkins, cabbages, everything off the train and everything was fresh. At Wirraminna, we had a garden there too, carrots, cabbages and grapes. Everything was growing in that garden. We were allowed to help ourselves.

After that I lived at Port Augusta for a while. I met Edgar Dingaman and I lived with him for about six or seven years and we went to Roxby Downs and he got a job there, so we stayed there for about one year, that's where my other daughter Isobel was born and I had two other daughters named Lorraine and Sandra, who were both born in the Port Augusta hospital. We went to Mt Vivian and worked there for a while, then Darryl was born in Kingoonya. After that we went to Andamooka and that's where my other son, Geoffrey was born. He's deceased now. We lived there for about three years, that's when I was looking after my father.

My brother Bill was out of the home then and was working in Arcoona and he used to come in for the week-end to Andamooka. I remember what he said to me once. 'What you looking after him for, because he dumped us way out bush,' but I said it wasn't his fault he left us. He couldn't live with an Aboriginal woman he was told. I used to ask Bill to chop wood for dad, but he never used to like doing it because he thought dad just dumped us, but he never. Then my father got sick, so I sent him down to Port Augusta on the plane. He went into hospital there and that's when he passed away. After that my mum got real sick, so I took her down to Port Augusta and mum was getting worse. I think she had something wrong with her lungs because they put this big needle into her back and drew some stuff out of it, then after that she got real skinny, then they sent her down to Adelaide.

When I went to see her she was losing her mind and I brought her back. I wanted to look after her but she didn't even know the kids — shame. I put her back in hospital and they sent her down to Adelaide again. When I went down after, she was really gone — like she was going mad.

When I first went down they were supposed to meet me on the train — sort of welfares I suppose. I didn't know Adelaide then. When I went there — just off the train — waited around there at the railway station and it was getting late. I walked across from the railway station to the hospital. I nearly got hit by a car. I didn't know the cars. When I walked across the cars came like this and like that. In the middle there they got that white square bit. I jumped in there and the red lights come on again and I took off and I bumped into one dark girl. She come around and I said 'Where's the hospital?' 'The hospital is just over there,' she said, 'Can you buy me a packet of cigarettes and a pie and drink and I'll go and show you the hospital' and I didn't know — first time I went to Adelaide.

She took me to the shop and I bought the things that she needed, so she took me to the hospital then — showed me where the hospital was and she walked away and left me. So I just walked around the hospital. I didn't know where to go in so I went right around the side of the hospital. I can't read the signs. I went to this little building there and I knocked on the door and someone come out. They said 'Hello, where you from?' I said 'I'm from Port Augusta — I'm lost!,' 'Oh, that's right — we were supposed to meet the train.' I went straight to the peoples — true.

Must have been a long time now. I was only 33 then. And they was talking 'We was supposed to meet the train' — I said 'Yeah, I don't know Adelaide — shouldn't have done this.' They're sorry and everything, so they took me to see my mum then. I seen my mother there. She didn't know me. That's the time I picked her up and brought her back to Port Augusta and tried to look after her and she used to talk — sing out — scream — the ground is falling — used to sing out blackfella

154

way — falling down — bit like earthquake — she used to say. I couldn't sleep for about three weeks trying to straighten her, to come back to her senses. She still wasn't ready though. The ladies out at the mission there took her back to the hospital in Adelaide. She died down there and was buried there too because I couldn't bring her back to Port Augusta and bury her there, I had no money. At that time we used to get rations. The only money I used to get was $23 dollars every month, it was child endowment. I tried and tried to get someone to help me but no-one would. Then after that I was really lost so Mrs Simmons gave me a house at the reserve in Port Augusta, so I stayed there with all my children. I got baptized in Port Augusta Mission and I lived there and had a good life with all my Christian brothers and sisters. All the Umeewarra Mission mob.

That's when I met Bob Dare, he was younger than me, but he was a gentleman, he helped me a lot with all my children, but he used to drink now and then. I used to tell him, 'Why don't you stop drinking?' I used to still go to church and he used to come with me. I used to feel inside that it was wrong, I was a christian and he wasn't. After that we had three kids, Maria, Robert and Colleen. I used to tell him to go away and forget about me, because my life wasn't the same. He used to get drunk and annoy me and that's when I started to drink as well, so we lived together and started fighting. Oh boy, did we fight. I was getting a bit rough with him. The devil really got me then. So one day I went to Mr Mac and had a talk with him and asked 'Can you help me to find a place out of the reserve?' So he put me out at Stirling in one of the places that he owns. So then I lived there for a while, but Bob used to come out there to see us.

I stopped drinking for good when I went out there but he kept on going. We weren't really living together. He used to come and go. He kept on drinking until he got really sick. Even the doctors tried to tell him but he wouldn't listen, so then he passed on as well. I lived with Bob longer than the other two. I still miss him today, never mind, we had fun living together. I am glad today that I moved out of the reserve and went to Stirling to live. Otherwise, I probably wouldn't be telling this story. I thank the Lord for this today, that he helped me through the years. He's the only one who can help. Jesus is the only way friends. I had twelve children altogether, six boys and six girls. Altogether I have thirty-seven grandchildren and three great grandchildren.

If I go out now, I like to have a tent or house. We went to Ernabella to see my mum's people. They wanted me to go back and see them. We saw them and my uncle's son. They had a house and they don't live in that house. They all live under wiltja. They don't use that house and they told me you can have that house there if you come back here. It was really good too, it had a stove, shower, everything in there. They make a fire outside and cook, damper and tea and that. They're frightened to use the house.

Jenny Grace

Jenny grew up travelling the River Murray with her parents, Ngarrindjeri people, living in make-shift shelters, and trapping water rats in order to sell their skins. They also fished for Murray cod and other fish in season and settled semi-permanently in a home made shack at Nildottie near Swan Reach. Jenny is now part way through her study to become a teacher and is based at the Lower Murray Nungas' Club at Murray Bridge.

Murray River Woman

I grew up on the Murray River near Nildottie. My father was a fisherman during the open season on Murray cod, and the rest of the year we'd spend travelling by boat between Renmark and Wellington trapping water rats for a living.

My parents always feared the welfare coming and finding us living in an old shack so I think that was one of the reasons that we kept moving — we had a little boat and we'd load it up with all of our stores, like flour and things. Most of the room would have been taken up with the boards, and I would have to sit on top of them. These boards were used for pegging out rat skins.

We'd just travel around, maybe row about seven miles, camp near where there was a big swamp or something, where we thought it was going to be good for rats. I think dad had about 120 traps and they would have been the most valuable possessions that we had. That was how we made money — we couldn't get money from anywhere else. We'd set out the traps and then after we'd brought in the rats we'd skin them and dry them. We'd stay in one place for about three days usually, until the skins dried, and if we ran out of boards to peg them on we'd peg them onto the gumtrees then roll them up ready to be sold.

If there was one place we thought was trapped out, we'd move along a bit further, maybe another seven miles and camp again. We'd stay in wurlies, even in the winter time. I can remember going to bed, muddy feet, walking in the mud then you'd go and just climb into the blankets but I didn't mind then. Dad made the wurlies out of tobacco tree limbs and old wheat bags that were pegged together with nails and he wrapped them around the branches and it wouldn't take him long to put them up. In about five minutes, he'd have a hut ready and mum would be out cooking something for tea and I'd usually be going to have a look around at the place.

We ate ducks and swans, and their eggs, fish, caught yabbies now and then, and there were plenty of rabbits around, especially during flood time. We would just grab them out of the lignum bushes, where they sat trying to escape the rising water.

We had a dog with us who sat on top of the boards with me when we were rowing on the river. Often me and the dog would go out collecting eggs and rabbits and whatever to eat and had great fun.

We would just throw ducks or fish on the coals to cook but eggs we would boil. Sometimes we cooked them in the ashes, I think that was the smaller ones, not the swan eggs. Sometimes we felt like a change and dad would catch some fish or ducks and trade them to the farmers. They would exchange clothes, or tobacco, or flour, or meat and cream and milk but most of the time we lived on damper, just damper and meat and fish so it was a treat to get cream.

I don't even remember eating any vegetables, I don't think we had anything like that, just meat and damper and fish. Maybe some times farmers would give us vegetables, potatoes or cabbage. When we were near a farm and camped not far away, there was usually an argument about who was going to do the trading. I was scared of dogs but my father used to explain to me that they were sheep dogs and they wouldn't hurt. Then he'd threaten me and say, 'Alright then, I'll go and you stay here and don't ask for any cream or anything when I come back or any clothes or anything that they give us,' so I'd finish up going by myself. Sometimes the farmers would invite me in and give me biscuits or something while they packed the box of things.

The clothes were not all flashy things and when I did go to school I used to wear some of them. Now thinking about it, it was embarrassing because they were usually old women's clothes and they'd give us shoes, high heeled shoes too.

Sometimes the paddle boats going past, like maybe

the *Coonawarra*, they'd drop off clothes as they went past and sometimes they'd stop. When we were at Nildottie they'd come past and sometimes buy fish from my father. They'd start tooting when they were way up around the bend and we would be starting to clean the fish ready. It was probably cod and callop. He used to catch all sorts of fish like callop, bream and catfish.

He used nets, lines, drop lines and springers. Springers were things set up on the cliffs with a big long stick. He used to make those with a branch of young gums which are real springy, he'd tie a piece of cord on it and on the hook he'd put a sort of a gold fish that would swivel around. He caught many cod on them. I think the main way he caught fish was with the drop lines. He had a shotgun for the ducks.

There were snakes sometimes. Once one dropped in the boat. We were lucky we were close to land, we just got out but I remember one of my Dad's cousins, he was telling me he was fishing underneath a willow and a snake dropped in the boat so he picked up his gun and shot a hole through the bottom of the boat. He must have been in that much of a panic, he didn't know what he was doing. We weren't really scared of snakes, like now I do worry about them, but then we used to walk through grasses and all sorts and not worry about them — probably lucky we didn't get bitten.

At night we'd all just roll in together and go to sleep. In winter time it was probably about six o'clock, as soon as it got dark. At day break, dad would get up and collect his traps and mum would make a fire. I'd go out and collect wood or boughs, to keep the fire going for breakfast and then if we were moving on that day we'd just pack everything up and leave.

We had no lamp, just used fire light. Later on when we were living at Nildottie we had a lantern, I think a kero lamp. The place at Nildottie was just an old tin shack. Dad found the tin along the river and then he just gathered it all up, old pieces of tin and made up a shack and we had bag on the floor. Mum used to put water on to make it hard.

We usually went up the river as far as Renmark,

trapping and would then come back to Nildottie and we always had our shack there, except for the time of the flood in 1956, I think it was 1956, one of the floods anyway, we come back and everything was gone, shack and the few little things that we had left behind.

After the flood washed the shack away, Dad looked around again until he found some more old materials to use to build another one, so he built it there in the same place and under the same little tree that he had the one before.

One time dad went out and bought an old Chevrolet utility. It wasn't very flash but we were all excited about it because it was the first vehicle we ever had. The next day we packed our few things into the utility and started off to Andamooka opal fields. A relation of my father's had offered to share his claim on a site there. I can remember we had a few breakdowns on the way up to Andamooka, nothing too serious that dad couldn't fix, but because of these breakdowns we spent about four nights camping along the roadside.

When we arrived there it was after dark so we didn't see anything until morning. I was up at day break the next morning anxious to see what this place was like. To my surprise it was nothing like I expected. There was only a few buildings above ground, one of which was a little hall that was also used as the school room. I also imagined there would be trees around but there wasn't one in sight. The most I saw of anything were mounds of white dirt.

Our place was a dug-out shared by my aunty and her three children. Because of the heat and dusty conditions most people lived underground. I can still remember how relieving it was to go down underground after being outside in the heat.

Dad started work digging mines underground. My mother worked as well, above ground, noodling, while I went to school. The school room was the only one shared by about fifteen students ranging from grade 1 to 7. I can recollect one friend there, a girl whose name was Joan.

The living conditions were very poor because of the

Swan Reach around 1930's.
A hessian covered 'wurlie' like that which Jennifer Grace lived
in while her parents travelled along the river for several months
of the year, trapping native water rats and living off the land.
Sheard Collection
SA Museum
© 1932

The Fletcher family at Swan Reach around the 1930's.
Jennifer Grace's home at Nildottie was made with similar
materials, i.e. flattened kerosene tins, hessian and other ma-
terial discarded by wealthier non-Aboriginal people.
Sheard Collection
SA Museum
© 1932

lack of water. About three times a week, in the evenings, dad made a bit of extra money carting water. He would go to a place not too far away with a forty four gallon drum on the back of the ute and come back with it full. People would be there waiting, wanting to buy a few gallons to wash clothes or whatever.

After about six months at Andamooka dad decided to come back to Nildottie and build another shack on the island. When we arrived back the first thing we did was jump into the river for a swim.

I sometimes go back up to Nildottie and like to have a look around where we lived, but there's signs up all over the place. I did go there at the beginning of this year to have a look but I was expecting somebody to come with a shotgun because with the signs there, I was trespassing. I wouldn't mind being able to go there for a good look around without sort of feeling under threat that someone was going to come there with a gun or something and tell us to get off. The time I went before I just went over in the boat and had a look around by myself but I've always wanted to take the kids up there to have a look and show them where we lived. There was just a bit of old cracked up concrete there — that's about all that's left there now — I don't know what dad had that for because I know it wasn't on the floors — the floors were just dirt and bag.

The first shack was just one big room but he divided it up after. We had an old wood stove put in while we were there but I was happy living there. I would like to live like that again if it was possible.

To get to school we'd row over the river and go up the hill. I think it was about 1959 the Nildottie school was closed down so we travelled to Swan Reach. Myself and a girl, whose father had cattle on the island there, she'd come down and come over by boat with me. Her father would bring her down on a motor bike and we'd go up the hill and catch the bus to Swan Reach school. When she was at school with me I was lucky because she'd give me all her old clothes and I had uniforms to wear like the other kids. Before that I'd be just dressed in old women's clothes. For about two years she came to school with me. Her father used to go with my father too when they were kids. They'd just cross over the river together and walk down to Nildottie school. They were different because her dad wore shoes and my dad had no shoes. Dad told me that because they didn't comb their hair, their father used to cut their hair off and leave a strip down the middle — like a mohawk style.

I had no interest really in school, it was boring to me. I always waited for the time to go back home. I was so different to the other kids there because they wanted to learn Maths and English and all that, but it didn't interest me because I didn't see it as having anything to do with the way we were living. I don't know about my father, I don't think he would've seen any value in school either when he went because they were just living on the island then doing the same thing, living off the land. I wouldn't have had any intentions of getting a job as a secretary or anything like that. I never thought I'd end up doing teacher training like I am now.

The only time Aborigines were mentioned at school was battles with Captain Cook. Everyone would just sit there in the classroom and spin around and stare and I'd just shrink down in the seat because it was embarrassing. Usually I was the only Aboriginal there except when one of my cousins was at school at the same time, but that didn't make much difference about the way I felt being Aboriginal. Most of the time I was by myself.

Purnong was one of the schools I went to. I remember one girl there went out of her way to make friends with me but apart from that most of the kids wouldn't have anything to do with me. My parents were embarrassed to visit the school. When I went to a new school they'd maybe walk me to the gate and from there I was on my own. I'd have to introduce myself or whatever and face all the kids and all that by myself, but I don't blame my parents for that because I know how they felt.

If I didn't have any money to buy my lunch I'd go without instead of taking food from home because that was another thing that was so different from other people. I wouldn't take damper to school or a piece of grilled duck or something like that so I'd go without,

165

and just wait until I went back home for a feed.

At recess and lunch I'd just stand around watching the other kids play. A lot of times I felt like joining in but they'd play their own games. Back then I think they probably didn't understand Aboriginals like people do now because white people are becoming more aware.

In lower grades I just kept to myself but when I was in higher grades I did get into a couple of fights. A lot of kids liked to annoy me by maybe just calling me names and I didn't know anything else but to hit them.

Sometimes I wagged when I was at Swan Reach school. I'd sit under a tree until I heard the bus go and then I'd run over the hill and sometimes go down by the river and sit for a while and go back under the tree at home time, in case my father was watching from the island. I'd just sit there and wait for the bus to come back and start walking back down the hill again. I only went to school because of threats of trouble from the welfare.

I went to Winkie school for a while. There was other Aboriginal children there then. At Andamooka there were other Aboriginal children too. I felt good there and I even remember some of the children there, like Joan.

When I was little I can't remember feeling the cold like I do now, living in a house, my feet freeze and yet living in a wurlie, I can't remember being cold even in the winter. Probably the mud kept my feet warm. We'd be in the water a lot getting yabbies too. In the winter time we used to go and crawl in the swamp for yabbies. We'd feel under the blanket weed and we'd find them under there. They must just sleep I think under the blanket weed and we would grab them, real big ones.

In the mornings we'd get up and light a fire and sit for a while and then go off and do whatever. When dad shot at ducks, he'd sometimes get twenty or so. I'd go out with the dog and both of us would be chasing the wounded ducks and that was good fun even though the water would have been freezing cold I reckon, but I liked doing it.

I don't think we wore very much clothes most of the

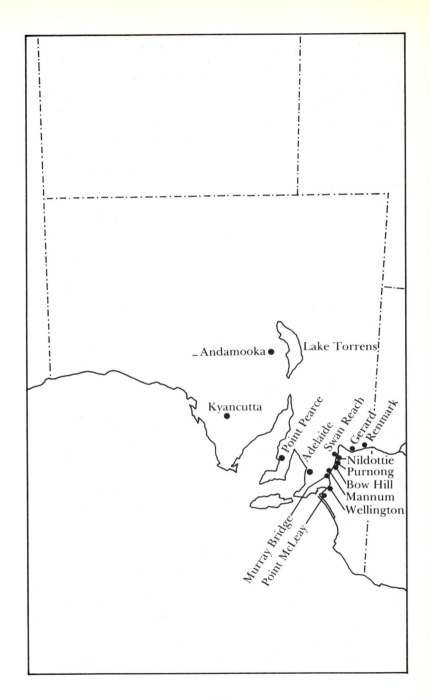

Andamooka • Lake Torrens

Kyancutta •

Point Pearce

Adelaide

Swan Reach

Gerard • Renmark

• Nildottie
• Purnong
• Bow Hill
• Mannum
• Wellington

Murray Bridge
Point McLeay

167

time. I remember we were living on the island when I was 13 or 14 and starting to develop when friends of dad's come over, some people I didn't know. He might have sold them fish, but he met them and brought them to the island, and I was there walking around with just shorts on. He was frowning at me as if to say, 'Go and get some clothes on,' when the fellas weren't looking. I was thinking what was he talking about because I had clothes on, I had shorts on, and I didn't realise. Now when I think about it I'm embarrassed because I didn't realise. He was saying 'Go and ask you mother, tell her to give you something to put on' because it probably happened all of a sudden. I didn't know what was going on because we had no mirrors to look in. These men didn't visit us that much but I had seen them before and I thought nothing of walking around like that. Most of the time up there, I just wore baggetty shorts and nothing else. I don't think I owned socks or anything like that.

If I didn't have any secondhand shoes, I'd go barefoot to school but everything was different there to the white kids. The shoes that I'd wear were probably them old plastic sandals or something like that. I can remember them. You could walk in the water and mud with them.

I was 9 when my mum had my brother. She went to Mannum hospital and he was born there. I was born there too. My father was born up at Nildottie on the island under a willow tree and I think most of his brothers and sisters were too. After my brother was born, my parents settled down for a longer time because it was cold winter time. We settled until he was probably 6 or 7 months old, then we started travelling around again. That was the time when I had to attend school regular in case the welfare came and took both of us.

I remember once the welfare did come but I took off for the day. I went off by myself up the island. Dad knew that they were coming and I don't know whether they came to talk or whatever but soon as they mentioned welfare, I was gone. Even my parents were scared of the welfare, but this time I think they had to see them because they found out that we were there.

That would have been about 1960 I suppose, but we were happy living there, even though it was pretty basic. White people couldn't see it like that I don't think. They couldn't see how we could be happy like that.

When we were living on the island one of my father's sisters who was married then, lived about a mile down stream and they also travelled around. They did a lot of rabbit trapping and rat trapping as well and they'd be gone a lot of the time. They had a shack too. A lot of the time that we were there they would've gone, or the other way around, when they were there, we were gone. Another one of dad's sisters travelled up the river doing the same thing. She was living close to Gerard and we went up there and stayed. She has one daughter living at Gerard now but my auntie died ten years ago.

We lived around Nildottie until my father was offered a job at Mannum, so when I was 17 we moved to Mannum, got our first house and dad worked at Shearers, making farm machinery, until he got too sick. Then he went on a pension because of his asthma, and he had heart trouble, but he worked there for a fair few years then died about five years ago. He was 56 when he passed away.

It was not too bad living in a house but altogether different to what we were used to, having people around and all that. My mum had been used to living like we'd lived before. She had trouble with how to do up a house, what to do, a lot of cleaning up. I think a lot of people who would have lived like that would do the dishes and that's it. It took time, she's a bit different now. It was hard for all of us because we were used to being by ourselves, not having anybody around. There were others in the family by then, nine of us altogether. One of my sisters died when she was 6. She had rheumatic fever. There's still eight of us, the youngest now are the twins and they're 18, in December.

The twins grew up in Mannum until my mum married again and moved up to Gerard. They're still with her at Gerard, and another brother who's 19 lives with her too.

I remember once when I was 9 I spent a fair bit of

time in hospital. I had a cyst on the lung and I went into Mannum hospital with pneumonia. My father was coming after two weeks in hospital, to pick me up on the Monday. But on the Saturday the policeman came and picked me up and the Matron explained to my dad that the police took me to Adelaide to the Childrens' Hospital because I had to have an operation. That was terrible for me; I suppose they thought I knew about the city but it was the first time I'd been there since I was about 3. I went down only once before with my father. The police took me down and dropped me off outside the Childrens' Hospital and I had a letter from the Mannum Hospital and they just said, 'Go in the door, they'll fix you up there.'

I jumped out of the car and I didn't know what to do. I just started crying when they took off because I was thinking, 'What is going to happen when I walk in the door?' Not only was I scared of not knowing where I was, I was scared about what they were going to do to me. I ended up going in there by myself and just standing there for a while, then I looked and I saw other people coming in and going up to the desk there and talking, so I went up and took the letter over to the lady and she said, 'Just take a seat.' I was sitting there and there must have been a hundred people in there and they were all sitting looking at me.

Finally after about two hours they called out my name from the doorway and I got up and went in. I sat for another hour or so before the doctor came in finally and they took me up to the bed. Then I stayed in bed and had to have an operation the next day. That was one time that I was really scared because I hadn't been to a place like that before.

I didn't feel so bad in the Mannum Hospital though. The Matron there was rather nice. I think I spent Christmas there and she bought me a Christmas present. But in Adelaide I was so scared, not knowing what to do. I spent three months altogether down there. My parents were too far away to visit me very often. Finally when I was allowed to come home, they told me I was going home on this day and I waited all day and the people who were coming to pick me up didn't turn up until about 9 o'clock at night.

I wanted to go straight home but they stayed a night at their place. The next day we left and when we went back my parents weren't at Nildottie they were at Bow Hill camping. I think my Dad might have been doing some grape picking or some sort of seasonal work there for a little while and they were just camped there. They visited me twice I think when I was hospital. After that I was alright.

I used to get ear trouble now and again, ear aches, swollen glands but because there was no doctors around you just put up with that. My dad was usually fit too. He used to ride a bike from Nildottie to Point McLeay which was over 100 km. I think his asthma might've been to do with where he was working in the factory.

There were times when we sold turtles and parrots for extra income to people who asked us to collect them. Looking back, I suppose it probably wasn't legal. One funny time I remember was when my dad said he was going to be real rich because someone was going to pay a lot of money for a pair of jackasses and he'd collected a lot more than one pair. The trouble was that he thought jackasses were grasshoppers but they had wanted kookaburras!

In the old days, white people used to pay Aboriginal people to collect leeches which the doctors used to use back then. Dad used to sell leeches to a man in Renmark who put them on his eyes for a condition he had. Mum once had a lump on her foot which stopped her from wearing shoes. She ended up putting a leech on it for just half an hour and she could fit back into her shoes again.

In 1963 I completed Grade 7 at Swan Reach school and in 1964 spent two months at Swan Reach High School but had to leave because my parents were unable to afford school costs. The only work we were able to do was seasonal so I worked with my father grape picking, pea picking or at whatever work was available.

I met my husband in Mannum and we now live in Murray Bridge and have three children, two of my own

171

and one foster son. My daughter is 18, my son 17, my foster son is 9 and has been in our care since he was 2 weeks old. I recently took on three more young foster children and have had to postpone my studies.

Notes on traditional life in Central Australia, the Flinders Ranges and the River Murray, Lakes and Coorong Areas

These notes will give the reader an understanding of the lifestyles, beliefs, values and attitudes of the traditional Aboriginal people from whom the storytellers descend.

All Aboriginal groups have much in common, for example, their beliefs in their Dreaming. Kinship relationships, spiritual beliefs, childraising practices, feelings for land, education for adulthood, technology and foods are and were similar but with regional differences. Languages varied widely although the languages of the north-west of South Australia were very similar, all being different dialects similar to Pitjantjatjara. The Adnyamathanha language is very different from Pitjantjatjara with only a few words in common, e.g. 'mai' for plant food. The Ngarrindjeri language is quite different again.

The main differences between the three regions, that is the 'Western Desert', Flinders Ranges and Murray River, Lakes and Coorong, include language, diet, clothing, artefacts and distance regularly travelled by those within the group. These differences reflect the climate, access to regular water supplies and resources available in particular environments. The Western Desert has a very low rainfall and is therefore sparsely vegetated. Consequently the people living there had to regularly shift camp over considerable distances. The Flinders Ranges is also often in drought but permanent water supplies were accessible and foods were usually in abundance so moving camp was a regular occurence but over lesser distances. Around the River Murray, Lakes and Coorong, there was always water available as well as fish, shellfish and an abundance of birds to eat. Semi-permanent camps were made in these areas and as it

173

was often colder, more clothing was worn. Clothes were made either from animal skins or woven seaweed or rushes. Little clothing was worn further north, although animal skins were worn in cold weather in the Flinders Ranges. Artefacts reflected the needs of the particular areas. Spears and boomerangs were common for hunting in the Western Desert. Clubs and nets were more often used in the Flinders Ranges. Nets, boomerangs, spears and canoes were used in the south. In all areas, women used grinding stones to crush edible seeds to make flour for baking. Dishes of various sizes were used for carrying water and other foods. Woven bags and digging sticks were used by all groups.

'The Dreaming is an all encompassing term that refers to what is known and understood. It is central to the existence of traditional Aboriginal people, their lifestyle and their culture, for it determines their values and beliefs and their relationship with every living creature and every feature of the landscape. It is the way Aboriginal people explain the beginning of life and how everything in their world came into being.

'Positive and negative human values are demonstrated in Dreaming stories as ancestors hunt and marry, care for children and defend themselves from their enemies.

'The Dreaming tells of the journeys and the deeds of creator ancestors who made the trees, rocks, waterholes, rivers, mountains and stars, as well as the animals and plants, and their spirits inhabit these features of the natural world today.

'It is the natural world therefore, which provides the link between the people and the Dreaming, especially the land or 'country' to which a person belongs. Aboriginal people see themselves as related to and part of this natural world and know its features in intricate detail. This relationship to the natural world carries responsibilities for its survival and continuity so that each person has special obligations to protect and preserve the spirit of the land and the life forms that are a part of it.

'These obligations may take the form of conservation practices, obeying the law, observing codes of behaviour or involvement in secret/sacred ceremonial activities, but the influence of the Dreaming is embedded in every aspect of daily life. The Dreaming permeates through song, dance, storytelling, painting, making artefacts, hunting and food gathering activities as well as through the social (kinship) system. It provides the framework for living.'[1]

'When a traditional Aboriginal person looks at the landscape, he or she always sees much more than just the physical features. There is a deep awareness of the presence of the Dreaming ancestors. All around are signs of their presence, their tracks, places where they had dug out valleys, split rocks or disturbed the ground in their passing. Sometimes too their bodies or those of their enemies are perceived in rocks, boulders and trees. Their actual spirits are also there, not dangerous or unfriendly, living on in the world they made. It is possible to communicate with ancestor spirits. This creates a bond of enormous strength.'[2]

'While the Dreaming may be viewed as a past era in which the creative activities took place and from which all life on earth has originated, there is also a sense in which all people have a direct link with this era through their conception. The people in each generation relive the activities of the Dreaming through their participation in daily and ritual life. Places and people today are conceived of as embodying the being of that era. People in the present are therefore considered to be in much more immediate contact with the creative period than is possible under a linear view of history. Aboriginal people did not place emphasis on the learning of family genealogies . . . They emphasized their closer links with the Dreaming ancestors. TGH Strehlow referred to the Aboriginal conviction 'that there was no division between Time and Eternity.' (Strehlow 1970:132)'[3]

'The Dreaming is still vitally important to today's Aboriginal people. It gives them a social and spiritual base and links them to a cultural heritage of more than 40,000 years.'[4]

Ruth McKenzie knows that her Dreaming is the Perentie Dreaming. Amongst other things, the Perentie

175

took all the women with light coloured hair westwards. This explains why many women in a particular area have blonde hair. Lorna Grantham grew up learning her Dreaming because she stayed with her mother's people. Muriel Olsson's Aboriginal father's Dreaming involves Ayers Rock. His name, Uluru, is that of the rock. Milly Taylor, like Lorna, learned Dreaming stories as part of her childhood.   Aboriginal law comes from the Dreaming. It explains correct behaviour as well as punishments for infringements of the law. Laws include how to relate towards various relations, rules for sharing of food, caring for the environment, who one can marry, who one has responsibilities for and obligations to. Aboriginal law, unlike Australian law, is not separate from religion, morals and ethics.

When children are born, they are continually told who they are, who their relations are and how to behave towards them. Children are cared for by an extended family, not just immediate parents, in fact, mother's sisters are also mothers and father's brothers are also fathers. A child will have many grandparents. Children learn by observation and imitation and their games help to develop skills needed later in life, for example, throwing small spears and clubs, learning to track small animals and identify plants for food and preparing foods to eat. Children are allowed considerable freedom when they are young and are not physically punished. Only when they are about to reach puberty are they expected to suffer the consequences of any wrong doing and punishments can be very severe. Many of the storytellers thought of missionaries as being very cruel because they physically punished small children, something they were not accustomed to yet which was usually accepted by Europeans. Children were also not told what to think but were given information when elders considered they were ready to receive it and they had to make sense of it themselves.

Girls were usually promised in marriage when they were very small. There were strict laws governing this. When boys went through the 'law' after puberty, they were usually told who would be their future wife. Some

176

men had several wives. Ruth McKenzie's stepfather had four wives. There are laws which involve people having to avoid certain others; for example, one would not usually interact directly with a mother or father-in-law but go through third parties instead. When listening to an elder, eye contact is avoided as it is considered inappropriate.

Music, art, songs, dances and stories were an important part of life. They were seen as ways of teaching as well as renewing life or ensuring success in hunting. Some ceremonies involved the whole community and sometimes outside groups as well, some were only for women and some only for men. Some were of a secret/sacred nature and others were open.

Men's roles differed from women's. Women provided most of the daily nutritional requirements, including plant foods and small animals. Men, either individually, in pairs or small groups, hunted for larger game, sometimes successfully and at other times, not. Important decisions were made by elders, both men and women, depending on the issue. There were no 'chiefs' or parliaments, although along the Coorong and River Murray, there were regular meetings of elected representatives who made important decisions. The occurrence of these meetings was directly related to density of population. Along the river and Coorong, the population was very dense whereas in the Western Desert, the population was sparse and most people lived in extended family groups. They came together as a community only for large ceremonial occasions.

Many Aboriginal people, especially in central Australia, still maintain the traditional lifestyles mentioned above but they now use guns for hunting, motor vehicles for travelling, western clothing, radios and telephones for communicating and learn English as a second language. Their values and beliefs still strongly reflect their understanding of their Dreaming, or Tjukurpa as they call it.

In the Flinders Ranges, while it may appear that the Adnyamathanha people live western lifestyles because they live in houses, speak English, work for and with

Europeans and children attend mainstream schools, the older people still speak their language, Yura Ngawarla, fluently and know many Dreaming stories relating to their country. They still take care to marry in the correct moiety groups, either Ararru or Mathari and eat traditional foods, animal and plant, whenever they can.

Further south, along the River Murray, Lakes and Coorong, traditional Aboriginal culture has suffered more extensively from the European invasion. However, there is presently a language revival push, some Dreaming stories are known as well and many aspects of traditional culture continue, including weaving mats and baskets with rushes and eating bush tucker. The Education Department of South Australia is presently writing Aboriginal Studies documents detailing the history and culture of both the Ngarrindjeri and Adnyamathanha people. Both documents will be of value in reviving and maintaining aspects of culture amongst those peoples, while also enabling non-Aboriginal people to learn and appreciate the histories and cultures of those groups.

1. 'Australia wide perspective', *The Kaurna people — Aboriginal people of the Adelaide Plains*, Education Department of S.A., Adelaide, 1989, pp. 27–29.
2. *ibid.*
3. Edwards, W.H., 'The Dreaming', *An introduction to Aboriginal societies*, Social Science Press, Wentworth Falls, NSW, 1988, p. 13.
4. 'Australia wide perspective' *ibid.*

Further reading

Bourke, C., Johnson, C. & White, I. *Before the invasion: Aboriginal life to 1788*, Oxford University Press, Melbourne, 1981. (Illustrated book on traditional life)

Edwards, W.H. *An introduction to Aboriginal societies*, Social Science Press, Wentworth Falls, NSW, 1988. (Comprehensive, easy to read text which includes some diagrams and photographs).

Education Department of S.A., *The Kaurna People. Aboriginal People of the Adelaide Plains: An Aboriginal studies course for secondary students in years 8–10*, Adelaide 1989.

Timeline of government policies and legislation affecting people in South Australia including the intentions and consequences

1834   **Foundation Act passed in British Parliament**

This Act made provision for 300,000 square miles to become the territory in which British settlers could begin the colony of South Australia. The territory was described as 'waste and unoccupied', thus denying Aboriginal land rights.

The Board of Commissioners gained power over the plans because the British Government wanted to bear none of the financial burden of the planned colony.

1836   **South Australia proclaimed**

HMS Buffalo party landed at Glenelg. Sir John Hindmarsh was appointed by the British Government as Governor and Commander in Chief of South Australia. He announced the beginning of British government in SA. No treaty was made with its original owners who nevertheless were proclaimed 'British subjects.'

Contacts were made only slowly with the Kaurna people of the Adelaide plains. These early contacts were cautious but friendly on both sides. The invasion of Kaurna land had begun. From the Adelaide plains, European expansion into Aboriginal lands, including land along the Murray River, Lakes and Coorong, as well as northwards, continued steadily.

In March, Stevenson was made temporary Protector of Aborigines in South Australia. The Protector had no power over land sales.

179

1837   **Aboriginal location established**

This was near the River Torrens near present-day Morphett Street bridge. Its purpose was to concentrate the 'problem' population. About 160 Aboriginal people lived there.

1838   **Aborigines Committee**

This was set up in May by Morphett and others to debate issues such as land rights. Early meetings of the Committee took a view that all land should be retained if obviously owned by Aborigines.

Payment for Land

Robert Cock paid three pounds, sixteen shillings and six pence for interest in land he had purchased, to go to Aborigines. Although a number of colonists made statements about the rights of the original owners, very few indeed actually made any such payment.

1841   **White settlement: Official and Unofficial**

After the land had been opened by overlanders and the main Aboriginal resistance crushed, settlers moved out to take up land. Some squatters moved ahead of official government surveys. The 1840's saw a number of conflicts, usually in the form of guerilla resistance by Aboriginal people. These conflicts centred on food resources and land use. Retaliation by the settlers against resistance often took the form of poisonings, whippings or shootings.

1842 **Waste Lands**

Land could be reserved for public use such as for the benefit of Aboriginal people. It aimed to encourage 'civilised' habits among the native population by settlement of an area of land for farming. This plan did not take into account Aboriginal lifestyle nor did it encourage their success as farmers.

Sections of land were set aside in the settled areas of the state only during 1842–1848. Most sections were leased to white settlers as the government thought Aborigines were unable to cultivate land. Twenty-four years later it was found that of the sixty reserves set aside, most were still leased to white people.

The Colonial Office in London ordered that a percentage of revenue from land sales now be reserved for Aboriginal welfare, as had been agreed to years before.

1844 **Ordinance 12**

'To provide for the Protection, Maintenance and Upbringing of Orphans and other Destitute Children of the Aborigines.' The Protector of Aborigines became the legal guardian of all children of mixed descent.

1844–9 **Aboriginal Evidence in Court**

Several ordinances were passed allowing the testimony of 'uncivilized persons', but the credibility of such evidence was left to the court's discretion. Previously, the evidence of Aboriginal people was not acceptable in court.

1860	**Select Committee of Enquiry into Aborigines in South Australia**

G.F. Angus testified that 'no subject in the course of the history of the colony has been so shamefully shirked as the welfare of the Aborigines.' No legislation followed. The enquiry was to ascertain whether the land and money set aside for Aboriginal people was justifiable. Most inquiries like this across Australia concluded (while not consulting Aboriginal people) that it was in the interests of both the Aboriginal and free settler populations to separate Aborigines from white society and isolate them on small reserves where they would be allowed to die peacefully, 'protected' from outside interference. This was the beginning of the Protection era which did not become officially legislated in SA until 1911.

Many people who gave evidence before the Enquiry expressed the opinion that local Aboriginal people were dying out.

1861	**Execution Law**

'Aborigines sentenced to death may be executed where the crime was committed'. This Act was not repealed until 1952.

1869	**Strangways**

This made it easier for settlers to gain land and it stemmed the flow of European settlers to Victoria where land was easier to purchase. It opened the flood gates on the rush for land in South Australia. This indicates the pressure on those sections of land set aside as Aboriginal reserves.

1911 **First Aborigines Act of South Australia**

The intention was to 'protect' Aboriginal people who were seen to be a 'dying' race.

The consequences were that many Aboriginal people were segregated onto reserves away from non-Aboriginal people. The law gave the Chief Protector power to remove almost any Aborigine to any Aboriginal reserve or institution and to keep them there indefinitely.

1939 **Aborigines Act Amendment Act of South Australia**

The Aborigines Protection Board became the legal guardian of all Aboriginal children.

The definition of 'Aborigines' was widened to include all Aboriginal people irrespective of 'caste' and whether or not they felt they needed the Board's 'protection'.

The Exemption Certificate was introduced which allowed certain Aborigines to become 'non-Aborigines' if they behaved as the Government wanted. If not exempted, Aboriginal people could not open a bank account, buy land or legally drink alcohol. Exempted people were not permitted to live on reserves and found it difficult to keep contact with relatives and friends.

White people were prohibited from 'consorting' with Aboriginal people unless they were 'exempted' from the provisions of the Act. Powers of expulsion, available to the Protector since 1911, remained and were used. This resulted in many defacto relationships ending unwillingly otherwise the white partner could be arrested.

1951   **Assimilation Policy**

The intention was for all Aborigines to eventually attain the same manner of living as other Australians and to live as members of a single Australia with the same customs and attitudes.

Many Aboriginal people regarded this policy as one of cultural and racial genocide.

Whereas previously, Aboriginal people were not allowed to live in town and were relegated to living in fringe camps, they were now expected to shift into town despite not being accepted by many white families.

1953   **Historic meeting held in Town Hall**

The Aboriginal Advancement League together with young Aboriginal people held a meeting to air their problems in gaining access to chosen careers and equal opportunities generally. Prior to this they were expected to work as servants or stockmen.

Atomic bomb tests at Emu

Two atomic bomb tests took place on 15 and 27 October at Emu in the north-west of South Australia. The land was considered uninhabited.Aboriginal people were not consulted. Those who could be found in the area were told to move. Some did not come into contact with officials and therefore did not know about the tests. This was not surprising as the affected area was several thousand square miles and only few officials were given the task of clearing it. Written signs in English were placed at a small number of places.

Walter MacDougall was apppointed as a Native Patrol Officer. He had red hair and bright blue eyes. He had the responsibility of looking after the welfare of all Aborigines whose life and culture might be affected by the Woomera rocket range. His patrol area was more than a million square kilometres.

MacDougall was previously a missionary at Ernabella. There was talk of him not being loyal to his Department. There was talk of communist affiliations and treason.

He was respected by the Aboriginal people who knew him because he obviously cared about them.

1956–7 Atomic bomb tests at Maralinga

Between 27 September 1956 and 9 October 1957, seven atomic bomb tests took place at Maralinga in the north-west of South Australia. Several Aboriginal people suffered terrible consequences as a result of the atomic bomb tests and those living have still received no compensation.

1959 Social Security Payments

The Commonwealth Government finally approved the payment of pensions, benefits and maternity allowances to all Aborigines except 'nomadic' people.

1962 Aboriginal Affairs Act

The power to remove Aboriginal people to reserves was abolished as were exemption certificates but the assimilation policy was still in place.

Having left a reserve, Aboriginal people had to apply for permission to revisit it. Offensive and petty rules and regulations still operated on reserves.

1964   **Integration policy**

This altered the policy of Assimilation where-
by Aboriginal people were encouraged to mix
in a non Aboriginal society but it did not
necessarily mean the loss of identity. Due to
much non-English migration, the government
recognized that Australian were not a 'homo-
genous' population.

1966   **Prohibition of Discrimination Act**

An official attempt to eliminate discrimination
in housing, employment and supply of services. Few if any successful prosecutions have
been made.

1966   **Equal Wages for Aborigines**

1967   **National Referendum**

This gave Aborigines citizenship and voting
rights to gain equality with non-Aboriginal
Australians.

Their inclusion in the census highlighted their
unequal position in Australian society.

1986   **Equal Opportunity Act, 1984**

Discrimination became unlawful in employment, education and the provision of goods
and services on the basis of race or ethnic
origin, disability, sex, marital status, preg-
nancy and sexuality.

Equal Opportunity does not necessarily mean
that people should be treated in exactly the
same way. Disadvantaged groups have particular needs which must be met to allow them
to participate fully in community life. The Act
allows for special measures like this so certain
groups can catch up.

The intention of this law is positive but until community attitudes change regarding racism there will still be many cases of racism by individuals and institutions and it is usually very traumatic for Aboriginal people to cope with this, let alone follow it up with legal action.

Adapted from the timeline as published in *Aboriginal land rights: (What do others think? What do I think?): An Aboriginal studies topic for sec. schools* Education Department of S.A. 1990

Lewis O'Brien, a Kaurna descendant, says his people had three laws to live by:
— Aboriginal traditional law by which his people had lived for thousands of years.
— 'European' law which applied to all Australians but which Aboriginal people had no say in, not even the right to vote.
— 'Protection' laws imposed on Aboriginal people which denied them rights such as voting and having any say over their lives and made them dependant on reserve managers for food, shelter and clothing.

Aboriginal people were denied basic human rights.

Glossary of terms used in the stories

Akurra giant serpent who created mountains, valleys and waterholes in the Flinders Ranges and whose spirit remains in parts of that country.

Bates, Daisy Daisy lived amongst the Aborigines at Ooldea and provided them with rations before missionaries arrived in the area. There had been a drought for some years prior to Daisy arriving so the people welcomed the rations. There was always permanent water available at Ooldea. Daisy wrote a book entitled *Passing of the Aborigines* because she believed they were a dying race.

business (Aboriginal English) term used to refer to secret ceremonies and initiations.

Davenport Aboriginal community adjacent to Port Augusta.

exemption a certificate issued to certain Aboriginal people from 1930 to the 1960s which included the wording:

. . . the Aborigines Protection Board, being of opinion that . . . of . . . by reason of his character and standard of intelligence and development, should be exempted from the provisions of the Aborigines Act . . . shall cease to be an Aborigine for the purposes of the said Act.

Without this certificate an Aboriginal person could not drink alcohol, open a bank account or buy land; with it, that person could no longer associate with his or her relatives who did not hold an exemption certificate because they could be charged with consorting.

hawker (English) travelling salesman.

he (Aboriginal English) he or she

humpy a wiltja (Pitjantjatjara) a shelter construct-ed of sturdy branches covered with leafy branches or nowadays canvas or plastic to make it waterproof.

ini (Yankunytjatjara) isn't it? isn't that so?

inma (Yankunytjatjara) ceremony including dance and song commonly, but often in-correctly referred to as corroboree.

Italyu place name, meaning not known by editor.

itjari itjari (Yankunytjatjara) commonly known as marsupial mole.

Kangaroo 1952 feature film starring Chips Rafferty and possibly Ava Gardner.

kapi (Yankunytjatjara) water.

kuka (Yankunytjatjara) meat.

kumpiti ghosts, spirits.

kumpurarpa (Pitjantjatjara) otherwise known as desert raisin or wild tomato which grows on a low bush.

mala (Yankunytjatjara) commonly known as hare wallaby which is now extinct in the north of SA; stories about the mala relate to Uluru (Ayers Rock).

mama (Yankunytjatjara) father.

maku   edible wood eating grub commonly known as witchetty grub.

malpa pikatja (Yankunytjatjara) promised partner in marriage
malpa = mate or companion
pikatja = soreness, beating or hiding referring to initiation business.

mamu   (Yankunytjatjara) devil, spirit of the dead, evil spirit.

Mapa   place name, meaning not known by editor.

mulku   native cat, quoll.

muntji   (Yankunytjatjara) fib, lie, untruth.

Nunga   the Adelaide area equivalent of Koori, meaning Aboriginal person of that area (Adnyamathanha) Yura (Pitjantjatjara) Anangu.

nyina   (Yankunytjatjara) sit, to sit, to live, to be, to exist, to stay.

nguntu   (Yankunytjatjara) you, 2nd person singular.

ranga   (Afghan) eye makeup.

sitting down   (Aboriginal English) to stay or camp at a place, when repeated it means stayed a long time.

tjilpi   (Yankunytjatjara) grey haired man, usually applied to an elderly male.

tjitji   young child or children.

turkey	(Yankunytjatjara) commonly known as bush turkey or bustard.
wanti	(Yankunytjatjara) leave, discontinue.
warnampi	(Yankunytjatjara) water snake, serpent in Dreaming stories.
watjilyitja	(Yankunytjatjara) half-caste, used in Daisy Bates time at Ooldea.
wiltja	(Yankunytjatjara) traditional shelter constructed with sturdy branches covered with leafy branches, canvas or plastic to keep weatherproof.
woomera	English spelling of an Aboriginal word for spear-thrower, it was adopted as the name for the Woomera rocket range in the 1950s.

Pronunciation guide for Aboriginal words used in the stories

Place emphasis on the first syllable of each word.

a	as in	but
e	as in	pet
i	as in	pin (in the middle of a word)
i	as in	happy (at the end of a word)
o	as in	pot
u	as in	push
tj	similar to ch	
th	like th in the, but without a puff of air	
p,b	as in English but without a puff of air	
t,d	as in English but without a puff of air	
k,g	as in English but without a puff of air	
ng	as in sing	
ly	as in William	
ny	as in news	

There are many other sounds in Aboriginal languages, too numerous to mention here. It is best to check with a speaker of the particular language to get the correct pronunciation.